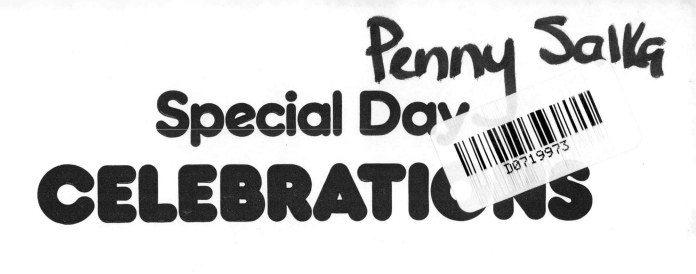

Special Days
CELEBRATIONS

Penny Salka

By Elizabeth McKinnon

Illustrated by Marion Hopping Ekberg

Warren Publishing House, Inc.
Everett, Washington

Some of the activity ideas in this book were originally contributed by TOTLINE Newsletter subscribers. We wish to acknowledge: Judy Coiner, West Plains, MO; Cindy Dingwall, Palatine, IL; Sandra England, Kirkland, WA; Ruth Engle, Kirkland, WA; Paula C. Foreman, Lancaster, PA; Peggy Hanley, St. Joseph, MI; Nancy J. Heimark, Grand Forks, ND; Colraine Pettipaw Hunley, Doylestown, PA; Barb Johnson, Decorah, IA; Joyce Marshall, Whitby, Ontario; Joleen Meier, Marietta, GA; Susan A. Miller, Kutztown, PA; Susan M. Paprocki, Northbrook, IL; Susan Peters, Upland, CA; Jane Roake, Oswego, IL; Kay Roozen, Des Moines, IA; Sue Schliecker, Waukesha, WI; Inez M. Stewart, West Baraboo, WI; Gail A. Weidner, Tustin, CA; Nancy C. Windes, Denver, CO; Jane Yeiser Woods, Sarasota, FL; Cookie Zingarelli, Columbus, OH.

Editor: Gayle Bittinger
Layout and Cover Design: Kathy Jones

ISBN 0-911019-24-3

Library of Congress Catalog Card Number 89-50765
Printed in the United States of America
Published by: Warren Publishing House, Inc.
          P.O. Box 2250
          Everett, WA 98203

Celebrate the Magic

Every day is special
When you greet the morning light.
Every day is special
When you gather in the night.

Every day is special
When you stretch to see the view.
Every day is special
When a child shares it with you.

Come and share the wonder,
Share the old and new.
Celebrate the magic
A child can bring to you.

Jean Warren, 1989

3

Introduction

Special Day Celebrations is filled with creative learning ideas to use for working with young children. Celebrations make ordinary days meaningful and fun. They allow children to focus on single topics, helping them to learn in ways that tie ideas and concepts together. And by serving as themes, celebrations provide children with a variety of activities that combine to create total learning experiences.

As you look through this book, you will find suggestions for celebrating fifty-five special days throughout the year. Included are familiar holidays such as Columbus Day and Mother's Day, holidays from around the world such as Cinco de Mayo and Lucia Day and days celebrating special events such as Snack-A-Pickle Time and National Clown Week.

For each celebration you will find an art activity, a song, a snack suggestion and a game or other learning activity. You will also find ideas for additional activities in many of the celebration introductions, which provide background information for teachers and parents. All of the activities are appropriate for young children and utilize materials that are readily available.

Below are more suggestions to consider for making your special day celebrations extra special.

- Expand your celebrations by incorporating ideas and activities of your own or let the children help decide on additional projects.
- Find children's books and stories that relate to your celebrations for reading aloud at storytime.
- Encourage the children to bring related items from home to share on your celebration days.
- Let the children make up their own "Piggyback Songs" to sing for your celebrations.
- Invite other children to come share your celebrations. Involve your children in the planning and let them help make invitations to send.

Contents

Spring

Summer

FALL

Labor Day

Labor Day falls on the first Monday in September. The holiday originated as a time to honor those who work and to give them a day of rest. Today, Labor Day is thought of as the last holiday of summer, and many people celebrate with family picnics or other outdoor outings. As part of your celebration, you might wish to set up a corner of the room where the children can look through picture books about community helpers and other workers.

Labor Day Mural

Set out a variety of kinds of magazines. Let the children look through them and tear out pictures of people at work (a person washing dishes, a truck driver at the wheel, a singer performing on stage, etc.) and pictures that illustrate different occupations (a police officer in uniform, a doctor in a white lab coat, a cowhand in western gear, etc.). Have the children glue their pictures on a sheet of butcher paper. Write "People at Work" at the top of the paper and hang it on a wall at the children's eye level. Then talk with the children about the kinds of work that the people in the pictures are doing.

Variation: Let younger children choose from precut pictures that have been placed in a box.

Labor Day Charades

Provide the children with a box of hats from different occupations (construction worker, firefighter, chef, baseball player, clown, etc.). Then let them take turns selecting a hat from the box and acting out what a person who wears that kind of hat does.

Variation: Whisper in one child's ear the name of an occupation such as "mail carrier" or "teacher." Then let the child act out what that worker does while the other children try to guess what the occupation is. Continue until everyone has had a turn.

What Will You Be?

Sung to: "The Mulberry Bush"

What will you be when you grow up,
When you grow up, when you grow up?
What will you be when you grow up?
(Child's name) will be a (name of occupation).

Let the children take turns telling what they want to be when they grow up. Then sing a verse of the song for each child.

Elizabeth McKinnon

Labor Day Picnic

Let the children pretend that they are workers. Make nametags stating their chosen occupations for them to decorate and wear. Then let them enjoy a "rest" from their work by having a Labor Day Picnic. Pack snacks such as sandwiches and boxed fruit juices in paper bags. Then take the children to a nearby park or other area where they can play after having their picnic.

Grandparent's Day

National Grandparent's Day is celebrated on the first Sunday in September following Labor Day. On this day, people express love and appreciation for their grandparents by giving cards and presents and by holding family gatherings. As part of your celebration, talk about the roles that grandparents play and encourage the children to tell about special times they have spent with their grandparents.

Decorated Bookmarks

Let the children make bookmarks to give as presents for Grandparent's Day. Cut construction paper into 2½- by 7½-inch strips. Have the children decorate a strip for each of their grandparents by dribbling on glue and then sprinkling on glitter. When the glue has dried, write the children's names on the backs of their bookmarks and let them stamp on their thumbprints. Then cover the bookmarks on both sides with clear self-stick paper.

Variation: Let the children decorate their bookmarks by gluing on pressed leaves or by attaching colorful stickers.

Flannelboard Families

Cut figures of older men and women and young boys and girls out of store catalogs or magazines to make sets of "grandparents" and "grandchildren." Cover the figures with clear self-stick paper and glue strips of felt or sandpaper on the backs. Let each child in turn choose a number of grandparents and grandchildren and place the figures on a flannelboard. Then let the child tell several sentences about his or her "flannelboard family."

Oatmeal Chews

Let the children help make cookies for Grandma and Grandpa. Heat 1 cup raisins in ¼ cup unsweetened frozen apple juice concentrate. Then purée the raisins in a blender. Mash 2 bananas in a large bowl. Add the raisin purée along with ¼ cup vegetable oil, ¼ cup peanut butter, 3 cups uncooked rolled oats, ½ cup nut-like cereal (or chopped nuts), ½ cup unsweetened carob chips, 1 teaspoon vanilla, ½ teaspoon cinnamon and ½ teaspoon salt.

Mix well and let sit for 5 minutes. Then press the dough into a greased rectangular cake pan and bake at 350 degrees for 25 minutes. When cool, cut into squares and let the children arrange them on small paper plates. Then cover the plates with plastic wrap for the children to take home. Makes 4 dozen squares.

Hint: Be sure to save some of the cookies for the children to enjoy at snacktime.

Grandma's Coming Soon to Visit

Sung to: "She'll Be Coming Round the Mountain"

Grandma's coming soon to visit, yes, she is,
Grandma's coming soon to visit, yes, she is.
Grandma's coming soon to visit,
Yes, she's coming soon to visit,
Grandma's coming soon to visit, yes, she is.

Additional verses: "She'll be driving a (new car/big camper/Mack truck/red scooter/etc.) when she comes; We will all be glad to see her when she comes." Repeat the song, substituting the word "Grandpa" for "Grandma."

Jean Warren

Johnny Appleseed's Birthday

Johnny Appleseed was born John Chapman on September 26, 1774. He was a peace-loving man who walked barefoot throughout the Midwest, wearing a cooking pot on his head and carrying a bag of apple seeds on his back. Everywhere he went, he planted the seeds or gave them away. Sometimes he stopped to help the settlers plant apple orchards, and when he needed new seeds he collected them from cider mills. As part of your celebration, you might wish to set out a basket of apples and let the children sort them by color or line them up from smallest to largest. You might also wish to let the children taste and compare different varieties of apples.

Paper Plate Apples

Let the children paint the back sides of paper plates red to make "apple halves." When the paint has dried, attach precut construction paper leaves and stems. Then let the children each glue a few apple seeds in the centers of the white sides of their plates. (Use seeds from other activities in this unit.)

Apple Seeds

Before cutting open an apple, ask the children to predict how many seeds there will be inside. Cut the apple in half horizontally and let the children observe the "star" that holds the seeds. Count the seeds with the children and have them compare the number with their predictions. Try the experiment with another apple. Does it have the same number of seeds as the first one? Try the same experiment using a different colored apple.

Extension: Set out apple seeds (with several of them cut in half) and let the children examine them with a magnifying glass. If desired, provide other kinds of fruit seeds for comparing.

Baked Apples

Make baked apples for the children to enjoy at snacktime. Wash 6 to 8 apples and remove the cores to ½ inch from the bottoms. Place the apples upright in a baking dish. To make syrup for filling the apples, pour 1 cup apple juice into a saucepan. In a small jar with a lid, shake together 1 teaspoon cornstarch and 3 to 4 teaspoons of the apple juice. Stir the cornstarch mixture into the apple juice in the saucepan and bring it to a boil over medium heat. Add ½ teaspoon cinnamon and ½ teaspoon vanilla and cook for 5 minutes, stirring often. Spoon the syrup into the cored apples in the baking dish. Then bake at 350 degrees for 1 hour. Serve with whipped cream mixed with a small amount of the apple syrup, if desired. Before enjoying their snacks, let the children sing "Happy Birthday" to Johnny Appleseed.

A Little Apple Seed

Sung to: "Eensy, Weensy Spider"

Once a little apple seed
Was planted in the ground.
Down came the raindrops,
Falling all around.
Out came the big sun,
Bright as bright could be.
And that little apple seed grew up
To be an apple tree.

Elizabeth McKinnon

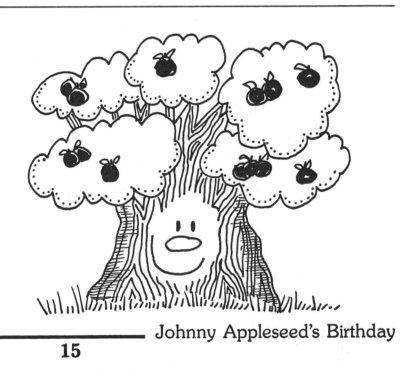

Johnny Appleseed's Birthday

Pickle Day

Snack-A-Pickle Time is the last ten days in September. Choose any day during this time to pay tribute to the pickle — the world's most humorous vegetable! Besides doing the activities below, you might wish to cut different sizes and shapes of pickles out of green felt and let the children use them on a flannelboard for counting, sorting and matching games. You might also wish to combine your Pickle Day celebration with a unit on the color green.

Pickle Puppets

Cut pickle shapes out of green construction paper. Let the children use felt-tip markers to draw on facial features. Let them also glue on green construction paper arms and legs, if desired. Attach Popsicle sticks to the backs of the pickle shapes for handles.

Extension: Encourage the children to name their puppets (Peter Pickle, Polly Pickle, Pickle Man, Pickle Lady, etc.). Then let them make up stories to act out with their pickle puppets.

Peter Piper

Recite the tongue twister below and let the children have fun trying to repeat it after you.

Peter Piper picked a peck of pickled peppers,
A peck of pickled peppers Peter Piper picked.
If Peter Piper picked a peck of pickled peppers,
Where's the peck of pickled peppers Peter Piper picked?

Traditional

Pickle Snacks

Chop sweet pickles and dill pickles into small pieces and place them in separate bowls. Let the children sample both kinds and compare their tastes. Talk about the texture and color of the pickles and about how they are made from cucumbers. Then make tuna or egg salad sandwiches and let the children sprinkle on small amounts of the pickles they like best.

Extension: Before removing the pickles from a jar, let the children try guessing how many are inside. Then count the pickles with the children to see if their guesses were correct.

Oh, I Wish I Had a Nickel

Sung to: "If You're Happy and You Know It"

Oh, I wish I had a nickel, yes, I do.
Oh, I wish I had a nickel, yes, I do.
Oh, I wish I had a nickel
So that I could buy a pickle.
Oh, I wish I had a nickel, yes, I do.

I would gobble up that pickle, yes, I would.
I would gobble up that pickle, yes, I would.
I would munch and munch and munch
While I listened to it crunch.
I would gobble up that pickle, yes, I would.

Elizabeth McKinnon

Sukkot

Sukkot, or the Festival of Booths, is a Jewish celebration that takes place in September or October. It is a time of giving thanks for a bountiful harvest. One of the customs of Sukkot is to build a harvest booth, or *sukkah,* in a place outside the house. The sukkah is decorated with harvest fruits, and a roof is made by placing green tree branches across the top. During the week-long festival, family members often gather inside the sukkah to eat their meals.

It Is Harvest Time
Sung to: "Ten Little Indians"

Gather up the food and put it in your basket,
Gather up the food and put it in your basket,
Gather up the food and put it in your basket.
It is harvest time.

Additional verses: "Gather up the corn; the grapes; the pumpkins; the apples; the nuts; the carrots; the berries," etc. Have the children stand in a circle. As you sing each verse, let a different child stand in the middle of the circle with a basket and act out the movements described in the song.

Jean Warren

Making a Sukkah

Let the children help create a sukkah for your celebration. To make a three-sided booth, place two chairs against a wall, about four feet apart, with their backs facing each other. Make a "roof of branches" by stringing green crepe paper streamers between the tops of the two chairs. Let the children make harvest collages by tearing pictures of fruits and vegetables out of seed catalogs and gluing them on construction paper. Tape the collages inside the booth for decorations. Then let the children take turns using the sukkah as a special place to eat their snacks.

Variation: Use a large appliance carton for your sukkah and let the children help decorate it.

Harvest Snacks

At snacktime discuss foods that are harvested. Set out bowls of foods such as nuts, seeds, dried fruits and raw vegetables. Let each child place a small amount from each bowl into a recloseable plastic sandwich bag. Help the children seal their bags. Then let them take turns enjoying their harvest snacks inside your sukkah.

Harvest Game

Have the children sit in a circle. Give them each a fruit or a vegetable to hold (or use pictures cut from magazines). To play the game, ask each child in turn to name the fruit or vegetable he or she is holding, stand up and place it in a harvest basket in the middle of the circle. Then pass around the basket and let each child choose a different fruit or vegetable to hold for the next round of the game. Continue playing as long as interest lasts.

Pizza Day

Choose any day in October to celebrate Pizza Festival Time Month. Pizza originated in Italy, but today it is an international favorite. Not only is pizza delicious, it's nutritious too. A pizza made with meat and vegetable toppings provides foods from each of the four major food groups. Besides doing the activities below, you might wish to purchase pizza stickers to use for making matching, sorting and counting games.

I Wish I Were a Pepperoni Pizza

Sung to: "The Oscar Mayer Theme Song"

Oh, I wish I were a pepperoni pizza,
That is what I'd truly like to be.
For if I were a pepperoni pizza,
Everyone would be in love with me!

Additional verses: "Oh, I wish I were a cheese and sausage pizza; an olive and mushroom pizza," etc. Let the children take turns naming their favorite kinds of pizza and singing about them.

Jean Warren

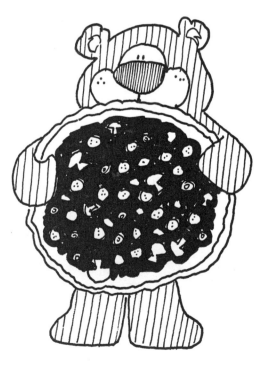

Small, Medium and Large

Make three pizzas out of posterboard, one small, one medium and one large. Talk with the children about the differences in size. Then one at a time, give the children sets of three objects in small, medium and large sizes (stuffed animals, toy cars, paper pumpkin shapes, etc.). Have them sort the objects by placing them next to the matching sized pizzas.

Collage Pizzas

Make paint by mixing red powder tempera with liquid starch. Cut various kinds of pizza topping shapes out of colored construction paper (brown pepperoni circles, black olive ovals, yellow pineapple wedges, green pepper rings, tan mushroom slices, etc.). Pour yellow cornmeal into a shaker container. Give each child a pizza wheel (or a circle cut out of cardboard). Have the children brush the red paint "tomato sauce" generously over their pizza wheels. Then let them arrange the pizza topping shapes on top of the wet paint and sprinkle on yellow cornmeal for cheese.

Mini Pizzas

Prepare a variety of pizza toppings. Include tomato sauce and cheese plus any other toppings the children might like (olives, mushrooms, cooked sausage, etc.). Have the children place refrigerator biscuits on a cookie sheet and press them out flat to make mini pizza crusts. Then let them spoon on their choice of toppings. Bake the pizzas at 400 degrees for 10 minutes.

Variation: Use toasted English muffin halves instead of refrigerator biscuits. Place the pizzas under a broiler until the cheese is hot and bubbly.

Alphabet Day

Children in Korea celebrate Alphabet Day on October 9. At school, instead of having regular classes, they take part in calligraphy contests in which prizes are awarded for the most beautiful writing. The holiday commemorates King Sejong, who developed the Korean alphabet for his people in 1446. Before that time, Chinese characters were used to write the language, which required learning a different character for each separate word.

Decorated Alphabet Letters

Cut the first letter of each child's name out of construction paper. Let the children decorate their letters by brushing on glue and then sprinkling on glitter. When the glue has dried, attach each child's letter to a sheet of construction paper and write out the remaining letters of his or her name with a felt-tip marker. Then display the papers on a wall or a bulletin board.

Variation: Instead of using glitter, let the children glue small pieces torn from colored tissue paper all over their letters.

Alphabet Song

Sung to: "Three Blind Mice"

A, B, C — A, B, C.
Sing with me — A, B, C.
A is for Apples we love to eat,
B is for Boots we wear on our feet,
C is for Candy that tastes so sweet.
A, B, C — A, B, C.

Elizabeth McKinnon

Alphabet Snacks

At snacktime serve canned alphabet soup. Or serve alphabet breakfast cereal or canned alphabet pasta.

Variation: Try this idea for making your own alphabet soup. Cook alphabet pasta according to the package directions and drain it in a colander. Pour chicken broth into a saucepan and bring it to a boil over medium heat. Then add the cooked pasta and simmer the broth for a few minutes before serving.

Alphabet Puzzles

Assemble 26 index cards to make a set of alphabet puzzles. Use a felt-tip marker to print upper-case letters on the left-hand sides of the cards and corresponding lower-case letters on the right-hand sides. Cut each card into two puzzle pieces. Then mix up the pieces and let the children put the puzzles together by matching the upper- and lower-case letters

Variation: Cut 26 identical shapes (teddy bears, pumpkins, etc.) out of colored posterboard and use them in place of the index cards.

Columbus Day

October 12 is the anniversary of the day Christopher Columbus discovered America in 1492. On August 3 of that year, he set sail from Spain with three ships — the Niña, the Pinta and the Santa Maria. Columbus believed that by sailing west he would find a shorter trade route to the East Indies. Instead, he landed on the island of San Salvador in the Bahamas. Today, Columbus Day is officially celebrated on the second Monday of October.

Land Ahoy!

Make telescopes for the children to use to "search for land" while pretending to sail on the ocean. For each telescope you will need two cardboard tubes, one narrow enough to fit inside the other. Slip the wider tube over the narrower one. Then demonstrate how to use the telescope by looking through the narrower tube and moving the wider tube back and forth over it. While the children are playing with their telescopes, recite the following poem:

Land ahoy! Land ahoy!
Shouts the sailor with great joy.
Land ahoy! Within my sight!
Land ahoy! We sleep tonight!
Land ahoy! It's good to see
Something other than blue sea!

Jean Warren

Variation: Use single cardboard tubes for telescopes and let the children paint them black.

Columbus Sailed Over the Ocean

Sung to: "My Bonnie Lies Over the Ocean"

Columbus sailed over the ocean,
Columbus sailed over the sea.
Columbus discovered America,
But Columbus didn't see me!
Niña, Pinta,
The Santa Maria, too.
They all sailed
Over the ocean blue.

Columbus was looking for India,
But Columbus missed it, you see.
Columbus discovered America,
But Columbus didn't see me!
Niña, Pinta,
The Santa Maria, too.
They all sailed
Over the ocean blue.

Karen Anderson
Pamela Barksdale
Barrington, NH

Columbus Day Ships

Give each child a walnut shell half, a small piece of playdough, a toothpick and a small square of white paper for a sail. Let the children decorate their sails and glue them to their toothpicks. (Or attach the sails as described in the Deviled Egg Ships activity below.) Have the children roll their playdough pieces into balls and place them in their walnut halves. Then have them stick their toothpick sails into the playdough to complete their ships.

Extension: Let the children have fun floating their Columbus Day ships in a tub of water.

Deviled Egg Ships

Peel hard-boiled eggs and cut them in half lengthwise. Remove the yolks and let the children mash them in a bowl with mayonnaise and a small amount of mustard. Spoon the yolk mixture back into the egg whites. Make a sail for each ship by poking two holes in a small square of paper and sticking a toothpick in one hole and out the other. Then insert the toothpick sails in the deviled egg halves.

Variation: Instead of making deviled eggs, use plain hard-boiled egg halves to create the ships.

Popcorn Day

Celebrate National Popcorn Poppin' Month by having Popcorn Day any time during October. Popcorn has had a long history in our country. The American Indians used it for food as well as for decorations in necklaces and headdresses. At the first Thanksgiving they introduced popcorn to the Pilgrims, who later enjoyed eating it with milk and sugar. What makes popcorn pop? Inside each kernel is a tiny pocket of water. When the water becomes hot, it expands so much that it bursts open the hard outer shell.

Popcorn Popping

Sung to: "Old MacDonald Had a Farm"

Popcorn popping, oh, what fun,
Popping big and white.
We will wait until it's done,
Then we'll grab a bite.
With a pop, pop here,
And a pop, pop there,
Here a pop, there a pop,
Everywhere a pop, pop.
Popcorn popping, oh, what fun,
Popping big and white.

Elizabeth McKinnon

Popcorn Pictures

Let the children help make a batch of popcorn. Give each child a sheet of light blue construction paper and a large pan shape cut out of black construction paper. Have the children glue their pan shapes at the bottoms of their papers. Then let them glue pieces of popcorn "popping out of the pan" all over the rest of their papers.

Flavored Popcorn

Let the children help make popcorn by measuring out the kernels. Explain that 1 tablespoon of kernels will make about 2 cups of popped corn. When the popcorn is done, flavor small amounts with Parmesan cheese, taco seasoning and cinnamon for the children to sample. Then give each child some plain popcorn in a sandwich bag and let the child shake the popcorn with a pinch of the seasoning he or she likes best.

Note: Eating popcorn is not recommended for children under age three.

Pop! Pop! Pop!

Have the children pretend to be popcorn kernels and crouch down near the floor. Choose a child to be "It" and have the child stand in the middle of the group with eyes closed. Silently signal one child to hide or leave the room. Then as "It" says "Popcorn, popcorn, pop, pop, pop!" have the other children begin hopping around and changing positions. When "It" says "Popcorn, popcorn, stop, stop, stop!" have the children crouch back down and stay still. Then have "It" open his or her eyes and try to guess which child is hiding. If "It" guesses correctly, let the child who was hiding be the next "It." If not, let "It" choose another child who has not yet had a turn to take his or her place.

Teddy Bear Day

Teddy Bears have their special day on October 27 — the birthday of their namesake, President Theodore "Teddy" Roosevelt. To prepare for your celebration, invite the children to bring their teddy bears from home and have extras on hand for children who don't have their own. You might also wish to set up a Teddy Bear Corner where the children and their teddy bears can enjoy bear picture books, puzzles and games. For added fun, let the children have a Teddy Bear Parade and plan to read or tell the story of the Three Bears.

Fuzzy Teddy Bears

Mix cornmeal with brown powder tempera paint and pour it into shaker containers. Cut bear shapes out of brown construction paper. Have the children brush glue on their shapes and place them in shallow box lids. Then let them sprinkle the brown cornmeal on top of the glue and shake off the excess.

Variation: Instead of using the cornmeal and paint mixture, let the children sprinkle on dried tea leaves or coffee grounds.

Teddy Bear Games

Assemble a large group of teddy bears before playing the games below.

- Let the children count the total number of teddy bears.
- Ask the children to sort the teddy bears by categories (color, size, those wearing bows, etc.). Then have them count the number of bears in each category.
- Have the children make different sets of teddy bears (five brown bears, three white bears, etc.).
- Review the concepts of heavy and light by having one child at a time hold a different sized teddy bear in each hand. Which bear feels heavier? Which feels lighter?

Teddy Bear, Teddy Bear

Sung to: "Twinkle, Twinkle, Little Star"

Teddy bear, teddy bear, turn around,
Teddy bear, teddy bear, touch the ground.
Teddy bear, teddy bear, reach up high,
Teddy bear, teddy bear, touch the sky.
Teddy bear, teddy bear, touch your shoe,
Teddy bear, teddy bear, I love you!

Let the children act out the movements with their teddy bears as they sing the song.

Adapted Traditional

Teddy Bear Tea Party

Make or purchase bear-shaped cookies and let the children decorate them with brown frosting. Pour juice into a small teapot and set out small cups. Then let the children bring their teddy bears to the snack table to enjoy a special tea party in their honor.

Variation: Instead of serving cookies, let the children make "peanut butter bear sandwiches." Have them use cookies cutters to cut heart shapes out of partially frozen whole-wheat bread slices. Show them how to cut off the points of their hearts to make the bread resemble bear faces. Then let the children spread peanut butter on their bear faces and add raisins for eyes and cherries for noses.

Teddy Bear Day

Pie Day

Celebrating the art of making pies and the joy of eating them is the purpose of National Pie Day on October 28. Pies come in many varieties — fruit pies, cream pies, meat pies and more. Encourage the children to tell about their favorites. To add to your celebration, let the children make playdough pies and recite the nursery rhymes "Simple Simon" and "Sing a Song of Sixpence."

Circle Pies

Give each child a round pie shape cut out of light brown construction paper. Then let the children glue on small red construction paper circles to make "cherry pies," circles punched out of blue construction paper with a hole punch to make "blueberry pies" or yellow construction paper circles to make "banana pies."

Variation: Use red, blue or yellow circle stickers instead of construction paper circles.

Pie Puzzles

Cut three identical circles (about 12 inches in diameter) out of posterboard. Decorate each circle with a different colored felt-tip marker to make three different kinds of "pies." Cut one pie in half, one into fourths and one into eighths. Then mix up the pieces and let the children have fun putting them together in various ways to create three whole pies.

Variation: For younger children, set out the pieces for one pie at a time.

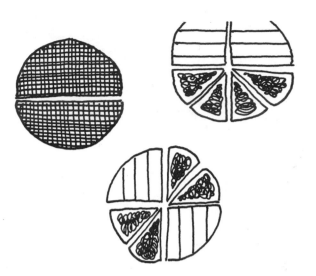

Favorite Pie Song

Sung to: "Skip to My Lou"

Lisa likes apple pie, my oh my,
Lisa likes apple pie, my oh my.
Lisa likes apple pie, my oh my,
Lisa likes apple pie, darlin'.

Andrew likes pumpkin pie, my oh my,
Andrew likes pumpkin pie, my oh my.
Andrew likes pumpkin pie, my oh my,
Andrew likes pumpkin pie, darlin'.

Ask the children to name their favorite kinds of pies. Then sing a verse of the song for each child.

Elizabeth McKinnon

Homemade Pie

Use a favorite recipe to make one large pie or let the children make individual pies in tart pans. (For a pie that requires no cooking, use a ready-made graham cracker crust and instant pudding for filling. Top with whipped cream.)

Variation: Let the children help make "thumb pies." In a mixing bowl blend together 1 cup flour, ½ teaspoon salt, 4 tablespoons margarine and 2 tablespoons water. Form the dough into small balls and make a deep thumbprint in each ball. Place on a cookie sheet and bake at 350 degrees for 20 to 30 minutes. When cool, fill the thumbprint holes with jam or jelly. Makes 16 to 18 pies.

Pie Day

Pasta Day

Plan to celebrate Pasta Day any time during October, which is National Pasta Month. Pasta is a favorite food everywhere. It comes in hundreds of different shapes ranging from macaroni and spaghetti to stars, shells and bowties. Besides doing the activities below, you might wish to let the children make pasta necklaces by painting macaroni and stringing it on yarn. Or have them make Halloween decorations by gluing pasta on posterboard pumpkin shapes and painting the shapes orange.

Noodles in My Soup

Sung to: "If You're Happy and You Know It"

There are noodles, noodles, noodles in my soup,
There are noodles, noodles, noodles in my soup.
There are oodles, oodles, oodles
Of the most delicious noodles,
There are noodles, noodles, noodles in my soup.

There are noodles, noodles, noodles in my spaghetti,
There are noodles, noodles, noodles in my spaghetti.
There are oodles, oodles, oodles
Of the most delicious noodles,
There are noodles, noodles, noodles in my spaghetti.

Elizabeth McKinnon

Sorting Pasta Shapes

Set out a muffin tin and a variety of pasta shapes (macaroni, wheels, bowties, etc.). Let the children take turns sorting the pasta pieces by shape into the muffin tin cups. Then have them count the number of shapes in each cup.

Variation: Set out a bowl of red, yellow and green pasta and let the children sort the pieces by color. (Or make your own colored pasta by shaking it in a plastic bag with drops of food coloring and a little rubbing alcohol.)

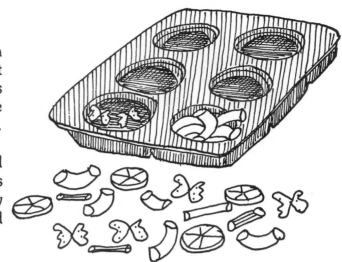

Macaroni and Cheese

Cook 8 ounces (about 2 cups) macaroni according to the package directions. Drain in a colander. Let the children help grate cheese to make about 1 cup. Reheat the macaroni in a saucepan with ½ cup milk, stirring constantly. Then transfer it to a large bowl and stir in the grated cheese. Makes 8 to 10 small servings

Variation: Let the children help make spaghetti. Or serve any kind of canned pasta.

Spaghetti Mobiles

Cook spaghetti noodles, drain them and allow them to cool. Pour glue into shallow containers and add drops of different colored food coloring to each container. Give each child a Styrofoam food tray. Let the children dip the noodles, one at a time, into the colored glue and then lay them on their Styrofoam trays. Encourage them to use as many noodles and colors as they wish and to arrange the noodles on their trays in any fashion. Allow the noodles to dry overnight (or longer, if necessary). Then remove the noodles from the trays, tie on pieces of yarn and hang them from the ceiling.

Hint: When cooking the spaghetti, add a little vegetable oil to the water to prevent the noodles from sticking together.

Sandwich Day

November 3 is the day for honoring that great lunchtime favorite, the sandwich. It is also the birthday of the Earl of Sandwich who, back in the 1700s, first thought of the idea of making a quick snack by putting meat between two slices of bread. As part of your celebration, discuss different kinds of sandwiches including open-faced, grilled, triple-decker and those made with pita bread. Encourage the children to tell about the kinds of sandwiches they like best.

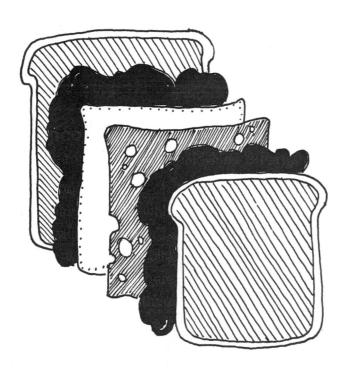

Sandwich Art

For each child cut two bread slice shapes out of light brown or white construction paper. Set out squares of pink and yellow construction paper to use for ham and cheese slices and slightly larger squares of green tissue paper to use for lettuce. Let the children punch holes in their cheese slices with a hole punch and have them lightly crumple their lettuce pieces. To make their "sandwiches," have them glue lettuce on both of their bread slice shapes. Then have them glue pink ham slices over the lettuce on one of their shapes and yellow cheese slices over the lettuce on their other shapes. When they have finished, put each child's decorated bread slices together like a sandwich and staple them along the left-hand side.

I'm Going to Make a Sandwich

Sung to: "Did You Ever See a Lassie?"

Oh, I'm going to make a sandwich,
A sandwich, a sandwich,
Oh, I'm going to make a sandwich
For my lunch today.
I'll put in some lettuce
And put in some turkey.
Then I'll sit and eat my sandwich
That I make today.

Repeat, letting the children substitute other words for "lettuce" and "turkey."

Elizabeth McKinnon

Sandwich Number Game

Cut fifteen circles, squares or triangles out of posterboard. Decorate the shapes with felt-tip markers (or glue on small food pictures) to make "open-faced sandwiches." Cover the shapes with clear self-stick paper, if desired. Number five paper plates from 1 to 5. Then let the children take turns placing the corresponding number of sandwiches on each plate.

Submarine Sandwich

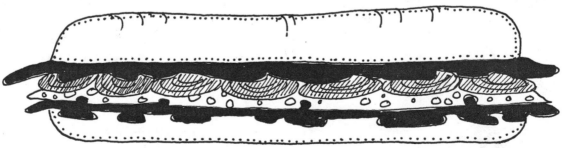

At snacktime let the children help put together a giant submarine sandwich. Cut a loaf of soft French bread in half lengthwise and set out a variety of sandwich ingredients (sliced lunch meats, sliced cheeses, sliced tomatoes and olives, shredded lettuce, grated carrots, mayonnaise, etc.). Let the children arrange the sandwich ingredients on top of one of the bread halves. Then put the loaf back together and cut it into individual sandwiches.

Homemade Bread Day

November 17 is Homemade Bread Day, a time for celebrating the joys of making and eating delicious homemade bread. Besides doing the activities below, you might wish to set out playdough and let the children experiment with making various kinds of "breads" such as rolls, bagels or hot dog buns. You might also wish to read or tell the story of the Little Red Hen.

Flour and Water Fingerpainting

Cut large bread slice shapes out of heavy brown paper bags or brown construction paper. Mix white flour with water to make a mixture that is the consistency of fingerpaint and add some salt for texture. Let the children fingerpaint with the flour and water mixture on their bread shapes. Then while the mixture is still wet, let them sprinkle on wheat berries (see the Learning About Wheat activity on the following page).

Hint: To prevent the shapes from curling while they dry, anchor the corners with heavy objects such as canned goods or jars.

Learning About Wheat

Purchase wheat berries (available at health food stores) and soak a spoonful of the grains in water overnight. At science time set out dried grains and softened grains for the children to examine with a magnifying glass. Cut some of the softened grains in half so the children can see that each kernel has a brown coat (the bran) and a white starchy center. Discuss how wheat is ground to make flour. Then demonstrate by grinding a handful of the dried wheat berries in an electric coffee grinder or a blender. Point out that the flour you have made is whole-wheat flour. White flour is made from wheat with the bran and the wheat germ (part of the starchy center) removed.

Extension: Let the children sprout wheat berries by sprinkling them on wet paper towels placed in small bowls. Enclose the bowls in clear plastic bags until green stems appear. Then remove the bags and have the children add water regularly.

Homemade Bread

Use a favorite recipe to make white or whole-wheat bread and let the children help with the kneading. If you've never made bread before, check a cookbook for step-by-step instructions. Be sure to start early enough in the day so that the children can enjoy eating the warm bread with butter when it comes out of the oven.

Variation: Let the children help make a quick bread such as gingerbread, banana bread or cranberry bread.

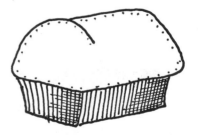

Making Bread

Sung to: "Frere Jacques"

Making bread, making bread,
Ummm, good. Ummm, good.
I can smell it baking,
I can smell it baking.
Smells so good, smells so good!

Making bread, making bread,
Ummm, good. Ummm, good.
Now it's time for tasting,
Now it's time for tasting.
Tastes so good, tastes so good!

Elizabeth McKinnon

Homemade Bread Day

Book Day

Plan to have Book Day any time during National Children's Book Week, which is the third full week in November. Many libraries celebrate the week with special displays and programs that invite children to explore the wonderful world of books. Besides doing the activities below, you might wish to take the children on a visit to your local library. Check beforehand to see if any special programs are scheduled for young children.

Picture Books

Make a book for each child by stapling four sheets of white paper together with a colored construction paper cover. Choose a theme such as toys and write "My Toy Book" and the child's name on each book cover. Have the children look through magazines and catalogs to find pictures of toys. Then have them tear or cut out the pictures and glue them in their books. (Let younger children choose from precut pictures that have been placed in a box.) As the children "read" their books to you, write their comments on their book pages, if desired.

Variation: Let each child choose the kind of picture book he or she would like to make.

Celebrating Books

Use one or more of the following activities for your book celebration.

- Set up a Book Corner where the children can spend time looking at picture books and telling the stories.
- Cut characters from a familiar story out of felt. Place the characters on a flannelboard and let the children tell the story.
- Read aloud a familiar story and let the children act out the roles of the characters.
- Make a set of story sequence cards. Let the children put the cards in order and tell the story.
- At sharing time ask each child to tell about his or her favorite story.

Cookbook Fun

Choose a simple recipe from a children's cookbook to use for making snacks. Set out all the ingredients and utensils that are called for in the recipe. Read the entire recipe to the children and point out each item you will be using. Then let the children help with the measuring, mixing and other tasks as you read the directions step by step. When you have finished, let the children enjoy eating the snacks they have helped prepare.

Storybook Friends

Sung to: "The Muffin Man"

Let's sing about our storybook friends,
Our storybook friends, our storybook friends.
Let's sing about our storybook friends
Who live down Storybook Lane.

Let's sing about the Three Little Pigs,
The Three Little Pigs, the Three Little Pigs.
Let's sing about the Three Little Pigs
Who live down Storybook Lane.

Continue with similar verses about other familiar storybook characters such as the Three Bears, the Three Little Kittens and the Gingerbread Man. If desired, hold up copies of favorite books as you sing the song.

Jean Warren

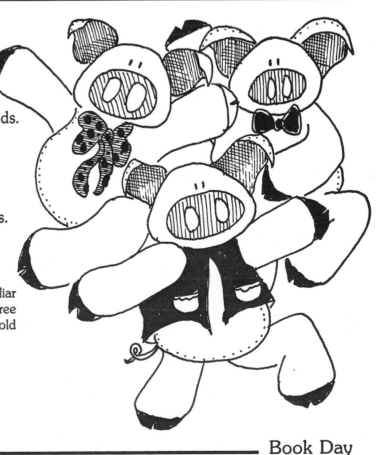

Family Day

Holiday time is a time for families. That's why the week in November that includes Thanksgiving has been designated as National Family Week. Choose any day during the week for your Family Day celebration. Besides doing the activities below, you might wish to display pictures of families and let the children make up stories about them.

Circle Families

Give each child a large sheet of white construction paper. Cut different sized circles from light colors of construction paper. Ask each child in turn to name the members of his or her family and give the child an appropriate sized circle to represent each member. Have the children glue their circles on their papers. Let them use crayons or felt-tip markers to add arms, legs, facial features and other details. (If desired, let them also glue on small construction paper triangles to represent pets.) Write "My Family" and the child's name on each paper. Then display the family pictures on a wall at the children's eye level.

Extension: With the children, count the number of people in each circle family and compare the number of adults to the number of children. Then compare the sizes of the different families.

Rock Families

Have each child collect four or five different sized rocks to make a "family." Then let the children play "house" with their rocks. Encourage them to make up stories about their rock families. For example, have them name their rocks and tell what each one likes to do. Or have them tell about how their rock families celebrate special occasions such as birthdays or Thanksgiving. Help them to expand their stories by asking questions.

Variation: Instead of rocks, let the children use different sized buttons or wood blocks to create families.

Family Cornbread

Talk with the children about how sharing household tasks is part of being a family. Then let them work together to make "family cornbread" for snacktime. Divide up the following materials among the children: 1 cup flour, 1 tablespoon baking powder, ½ teaspoon salt, 1 cup yellow cornmeal, 1 egg, ½ cup unsweetened frozen apple juice concentrate, ½ cup milk, ¼ cup vegetable oil, 1 mashed banana, a large bowl and a mixing spoon. Ask the children how they think they can use their materials to make cornbread. Once they have decided that they will need to mix all the ingredients together, let them do so. Then pour the batter into a greased 9-inch square pan and bake at 400 degrees for 25 to 30 minutes. Makes 16 small squares.

With My Family

Sung to: "The Muffin Man"

Tell me what you like to do,
Like to do, like to do.
Tell me what you like to do
With your family.

Edward likes to rake the leaves,
Rake the leaves, rake the leaves.
Edward likes to rake the leaves
With his family.

Let the children tell about things they like to do with their families. Then sing a verse of the song for each child.

Elizabeth McKinnon

Saint Nicholas Day

Saint Nicholas Day on December 6 is observed in several European countries, but the celebration in Holland is especially fun for children. Before the holiday they wait for Saint Nicholas, or *Sinterklaas,* to make his appearance dressed in his bishop's hat, white robes and red cape. On Saint Nicholas Day Eve they join with their families for feasting and exchanging presents, which often are hidden in unusual places throughout the house. Before going to bed, the children place their shoes by the hearth. In the morning they find that Saint Nicholas has paid a visit during the night and filled their shoes with small toys and sweets.

Saint Nicholas Day Gift Hunt

Make or purchase inexpensive gifts for the children (paper flowers, balloons, stickers, sugarless gum, etc.). Use a different colored or patterned paper to wrap each gift and cut a small square out of each kind of wrapping paper used. Hide the gifts around the room and give each child one of the paper squares. Then play music and let the children go on a Gift Hunt. When each child has found the gift with wrapping that matches his or her paper square, have all the children sit in a circle and open their gifts together.

Saint Nicholas

Sung to: "The Muffin Man"

Here comes dear Saint Nicholas,
Saint Nicholas, Saint Nicholas.
Here comes dear Saint Nicholas
With his big bag of toys.

He's bringing gifts at Christmastime,
At Christmastime, at Christmastime.
He's bringing gifts at Christmastime
For all the girls and boys.

Elizabeth McKinnon

Sinterklaas Graham Crackers

In a large bowl stir together 1 cup graham flour, 1 cup whole-wheat flour, ½ teaspoon baking soda and ½ teaspoon salt. Combine in a blender ¼ cup unsweetened frozen apple juice concentrate, ¼ cup vegetable oil, 1 sliced banana, 1 teaspoon vanilla and 1 teaspoon cinnamon. Add the blender ingredients to the dry ingredients and mix well. Roll the dough out as thinly as possible on a floured surface. Then let the children use Santa Claus cookie cutters to cut out "Sinterklaas" shapes. Poke holes in the shapes with a fork to add details. Place the crackers on a cookie sheet and bake at 350 degrees for 6 to 8 minutes. Makes about 2 dozen crackers.

Saint Nicholas Day Mural

Use felt-tip markers to draw a picture of a fireplace with a wide hearth in the center of a long piece of butcher paper. Hang the paper on a wall at the children's eye level. For each child cut one or two shoe shapes out of dark colored construction paper. Let the children tear pictures of candies, cookies and small toys out of Christmas catalogs and glue them on their shoe shapes to represent presents left by Saint Nicholas. Then help the children attach their shoe shapes to the fireplace hearth on the butcher paper.

Poinsettia Day

Poinsettia Day on December 12 is the day for enjoying poinsettias and for remembering Dr. Joel R. Poinsett, the man who introduced the native Mexican plant in the United States and for whom the poinsettia is named. As part of your celebration, you might wish to take the children to a florist shop or a supermarket to see the poinsettias on display. Point out that the bright red or white petals are actually leaves and that the yellow centers are the true flowers. (Note: Avoid letting the children touch the plants. Although poinsettias are not toxic, the sap can be irritating to the eyes and mouth.)

Poinsettia Planting Game

Paint six Popsicle sticks and the lid of a shoebox green. Cut six poinsettia flower shapes (about 3 inches wide) out of red construction paper. Use a hole punch to punch 21 circles out of yellow construction paper. Number the poinsettia shapes from 1 to 6 by gluing the appropriate number of yellow circles in the centers of the shapes. When the glue has dried, attach the poinsettia shapes to the tops of the green Popsicle stick "stems." Cut six slits in the lid of the shoebox and use a black felt-tip marker to number them from 1 to 6. Then let the children take turns "planting the poinsettias" by inserting them in the matching numbered slits.

Poinsettia Collages

Set out holiday wrapping paper and old Christmas cards that contain pictures of poinsettias. Let the children tear or cut out the pictures and glue them on sheets of white construction paper to make poinsettia collages. If desired, give them each a few poinsettia stickers to add to their collages and let them sprinkle on glitter while the glue is still wet.

Variation: Have the children make their collages on small paper plates. Then attach loops of yarn and hang the decorated plates as holiday ornaments.

Poinsettia Salads

Tint mayonnaise yellow by adding a few drops of food coloring. Slice ripe tomatoes into thin wedges. To make each salad, place a spoonful of the yellow mayonnaise in the center of a paper plate. Then arrange tomato wedges around the mayonnaise to create a red poinsettia flower. If desired, tuck a few spinach leaves between the tomato wedges to add a touch of green.

Poinsettia Day Is Here

Sung to: "The Farmer in the Dell"

Poinsettia Day is here,
Let's clap our hands and cheer.
Red and green poinsettias say
That Christmastime is near.

Alternate verse: Substitute the words "holiday time" for "Christmastime."

Elizabeth McKinnon

Lucia Day

Lucia Day, which falls on December 13, marks the beginning of the Christmas season in Sweden. This holiday honors Lucy, the "Saint of Light," who brings brightness and hope at the darkest time of the year. Early in the morning the oldest daughter of the house dresses in a white robe with a red sash to play the role of Lucy. On her head she wears a crown of evergreens topped with lighted candles. Then accompanied by her sisters and brothers, she carries plates of traditional Lucia buns and cups of hot coffee to all the adult family members, who are still in bed. As the children walk through the house, they sing the Swedish version of "Santa Lucia."

Lucia Crowns

For your celebration, let everyone make a Lucia crown. Cut the centers out of paper plates and have the children glue short strips of green crepe paper "evergreens" on the tops of the rims. When the glue has dried, poke five or six small holes in each crown and let the children stick white birthday candles (with the wicks cut off) in the holes.

Note: The candles on the crowns are not to be lighted.

Lucia Crown Number Game

Cut five Lucia crown shapes out of green construction paper and glue each one on a large index card. Number the cards from 1 to 5 by taping the appropriate number of birthday candles on each crown. Number five additional index cards from 1 to 5 with a felt-tip marker. Lay out all the cards on a table or on the floor. Then let the children take turns counting the candles on the crowns and pairing the crown cards with the matching numbered cards.

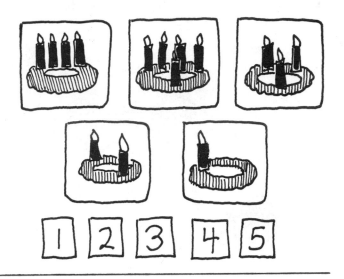

Lucia Day

Sung to: "Twinkle, Twinkle, Little Star"

Candles, candles, burning bright,
Filling all the world with light.
Now it is Lucia Day,
Time for us to sing and play.
Candles, candles, burning bright,
Filling all the world with light.

Elizabeth McKinnon

Lucia Day Snacks

Let the children help make this adapted version of the Lucia buns called "Lucia cats." Thaw one loaf of frozen bread dough and let it rise. Divide the dough into about 12 pieces and let the children shape the pieces into 8- to 9-inch rolls. Form each roll into a closed "S" shape and place a raisin in each curve of the "S" to make "cat's eyes." Place the buns on a greased cookie sheet and bake at 350 degrees for about 15 minutes or until the tops are golden brown.

Extension: At snacktime let the children put on their Lucia crowns from the activity on the previous page and pretend to light the candles. Then before they sit down to eat, let them walk around the room in a "Lucia Day Processional" while singing the Lucia Day song above.

Lucia Day

49

Birds' Christmas

Sharing the Christmas feast with the birds is a traditional custom in Scandinavian countries. At harvest time several of the best bundles of wheat or oats are stored away in a special place. Then on Christmas Eve the bundles of grain are tied to poles outside in the snow for the birds to find on Christmas morning. As part of your celebration, you might wish to hang a bird feeder outside a window of your room. Let the children help keep the feeder full of birdseed throughout the winter.

Bird Treats

Give each child a pinecone (or a cardboard toilet tissue tube) and set out small bowls of peanut butter. Let the children use plastic spoons to spread the peanut butter all over their pinecones. Then have them roll their pinecones in birdseed. When they have finished, attach loops of red or green yarn to make hangers.

Variation: Let the children make bird treats by stringing Cheerios on pieces of red or green yarn. Then tie the ends of each child's yarn piece together in a bow.

Bird Walk

Have the children bundle up in warm clothes. Then take them outside to find a tree or a large bush on which to hang their bird treats from the activity on the previous page. While they are hanging their treats, let them sing "We Wish You a Merry Christmas" to the birds. Then go on a walk to look for birds that are still in your area during wintertime. Talk about the different kinds of birds you see and encourage the children to look for different sizes and colors of birds. If desired, ask each child to count the number of birds he or she sees. Then total up the number when you return from your walk

Hint: Some children may wish to take their bird treats home to hang in their own yards.

Little Birds

Sung to: "Down by the Station"

Out in the garden
On a winter morning,
See all the little birds
Playing in the snow.
See them eat the <u>(seeds/crumbs/etc.)</u>
We put out for their breakfast.
Peck, Peck — Tweet, Tweet,
Off they go!

Let several children at a time pretend to be birds playing in the snow while everyone else sings the song.

Elizabeth McKinnon

Birds-in-the-Snow

Let the children help make these treats for snacktime. Cut celery stalks into short lengths and fill them with cream cheese "snow." Have the children place raisins on top of the cheese to represent birds. Then let them sprinkle on sesame or sunflower seeds for birdseed.

New Year's Celebration

New Year's is the time for saying goodbye to the old year and hello to the new. People celebrate with parties and parades and look forward to new beginnings by making New Year's resolutions. As part of your celebration, introduce the children to the new calendar. Let them make "New Year's resolutions" by naming new things they want to learn in the coming year.

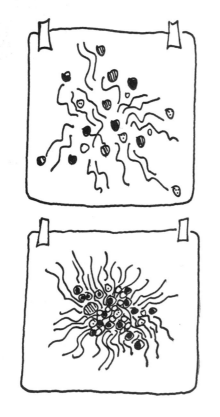

New Year's Collages

Make "confetti" by punching circles out of brightly colored construction paper with a hole punch. Have the children brush glue all over sheets of dark blue or black construction paper. Then let them drop strands of silver tinsel on top of the glue and sprinkle on small handfuls of confetti. When the glue has dried, display the collages around the room for New Year's decorations.

New Year's Parade

Make small cone-shaped hats out of construction paper and attach yarn to the sides for ties. Let the children decorate their hats by gluing on materials such as colored paper scraps, yarn, ribbon, tinsel and glitter. When the glue has dried, help the children put on their hats and give them each a rhythm instrument. Then play music and let them march around the room in a New Year's Parade.

Variation: Let the children sing the New Year's song below as they march and have them accompany each verse with the appropriate rhythm instruments.

Happy New Year

Sung to: "Frere Jacques"

Hear the bells, hear the bells,
Ding, ding, dong; ding, ding, dong.
Ringing out the old year,
Ringing in the new year,
Ding, ding, dong; ding, ding, dong.

Hear the horns, hear the horns,
Toot, toot, toot; toot, toot, toot.
Tooting out the old year,
Tooting in the new year,
Toot, toot, toot; toot, toot, toot.

Hear the cymbals, hear the cymbals,
Clang, clang, clang; clang, clang, clang.
Clanging out the old year,
Clanging in the new year,
Clang, clang, clang; clang, clang, clang.

Additional verses: "Hear the drums — boom, boom, boom; Hear the sticks — clack, clack, clack."

Elizabeth McKinnon

New Year's Party

Set the snack table with colorful placemats and add strands of curled ribbon for decorations. For snacks serve Sparkling New Year's Punch (recipe follows) with cookies or with chips and dip. Let the children sing "Happy Birthday" to the new year before enjoying their snacks.

Sparkling New Year's Punch — In a large pitcher mix together one 12-ounce can unsweetened frozen apple juice concentrate, two cans (24 ounces) cold water and one 32-ounce bottle club soda. Stir well and pour into clear plastic cups. Makes 17 small servings.

New Year's Celebration

Soup Day

When winter winds blow, nothing tastes better than a bowl of hot soup. That's why January has been designated as National Soup Month. Choose any day during January for your celebration. Besides doing the activities below, ask the children to tell about their favorite kinds of soup and discuss how dry soup mixes and canned soups are prepared. You might also wish to set out soup cans and boxes that have pictures on the labels and let the children use them for matching, sorting and counting games.

Pots of Soup

Cut large soup pot shapes out of brown paper grocery bags or any other kind of light brown paper. Slice vegetables such as carrots, potatoes, turnips and celery into thick sections to use for stamps. Make paint pads by placing folded paper towels in shallow containers and pouring on tempera paints (orange for carrots, brown for potatoes, white for turnips, green for celery, etc.). Then let the children dip the cut surfaces of the vegetables into the paints and press them on their soup pot shapes to make prints.

Variation: Let the children tear pictures of vegetables out of magazines or seed catalogs and glue them on their soup pot shapes.

The Soup Is Boiling Up

Sung to: "The Farmer in the Dell"

The soup is boiling up,
The soup is boiling up.
Stir slow, around we go,
The soup is boiling up.

First we make the broth,
First we make the broth.
Stir slow, around we go,
The soup is boiling up.

Now we add some carrots,
Now we add some carrots.
Stir slow, around we go,
The soup is boiling up.

Continue with similar verses, using other vegetable names. Have the children stand around a large imaginary pot and pretend to stir the soup as they sing.

Jean Warren

Color Soups

Make "bowls of soup" by painting the insides of four white paper bowls these colors: red, yellow, green and orange. From construction paper cut out red half-circles for tomato wedges, small yellow triangles for corn kernels, small green circles for peas and larger orange circles for carrot slices. Then place all the shapes in a shallow container and let the children take turns sorting the vegetables into the matching colored "soups."

Variation: Attach red, yellow, green and orange self-stick dots (or construction paper circles) to plastic spoons. Then let the children place the spoons in the matching colored soup bowls.

Stone Soup

Read or tell the folktale "Stone Soup." Then pour about 2 quarts water into a large pot and let the children put in a round smooth stone that has been scrubbed and boiled. Add chopped carrots, celery, potatoes, onions, zucchini and tomatoes. Bring to a boil and let simmer, covered, for about 1 hour. When the vegetables are tender, add instant broth or bouillon and season to taste. If desired, stir in small pieces of cooked meat or chicken shortly before serving.

Variation: Make ordinary homemade soup by omitting the stone in the recipe above. Or serve any kind of canned soup.

Martin Luther King's Birthday

Martin Luther King, Jr. was born on January 15, 1929. He was a clergyman and a civil rights leader who devoted his life to the nonviolent struggle for freedom and peace for all people. Dr. King had many dreams for his country. One of those dreams was that his four children would "one day live in a nation where they will not be judged by the color of their skin but by the content of their character."

Handprint Placemats

Martin Luther King hoped that all children, no matter what their race or religion, would someday be able to join hands and become friends. As part of your celebration, let the children make handprint placemats to use for snacktime. Give each child a large sheet of construction paper. Spread thick tempera paint on a sheet of heavy plastic. Then let the children place their hands in the paint and press them all over their papers to make handprints. When the paint has dried, cover the placemats with clear self-stick paper, if desired.

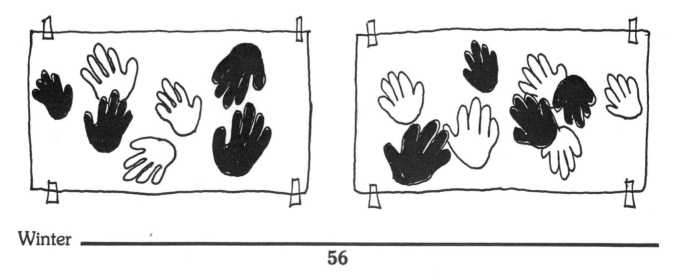

I Have a Dream

Martin Luther King is remembered for his "I Have a Dream" speech in which he wished for a country where all people would live together in harmony. Talk with the children about dreams, or wishes. What things could they wish for that would make our country, or our world, a better place for everyone to live? If desired, write the children's wishes on paper for them to illustrate. Then fasten the papers together with a cover to make an "I Have a Dream" Book.

Happy Birthday, Dr. King

Sung to: "Yankee Doodle"

Dr. King was a man
Who had a special dream.
He dreamed of a world filled with love
And peace and harmony.
Happy Birthday, Dr. King,
Happy Birthday to you.
Happy Birthday, Dr. King,
We love you, yes, we do.

Debra Butler
Denver, CO

Hand Cookies

Use a favorite recipe to make sugar cookies and let the children help roll out the dough. Have each child place one hand on the dough while you trace around it. Then cut out the shape and write the child's name on it with a toothpick. Bake the hand cookies according to your recipe directions and let the children enjoy them at snacktime.

Martin Luther King's Birthday

Hat Day

The purpose of Hat Day, traditionally celebrated on the third Friday in January, is to pay tribute to the many kinds of hats and head coverings that are worn all over the world. As part of your celebration, invite the children to bring in their favorite hats to show and tell about at circle time. You might also wish to make a number of cone-shaped hats in different colors and sizes to use for matching, sorting and counting games.

Decorated Hats

Make brimmed hats by cutting the centers out of paper plates and stapling paper soup bowls over the holes. Let the children decorate their hats by gluing on materials such as yarn, feathers, sequins, fabric scraps, ribbon and glitter. When the glue has dried, attach yarn to the sides of the hats for ties.

Variation: Turn the brimmed hats into caps with visors by trimming off the backs and sides of the paper plate brims and cutting the fronts into visor shapes. Or make cone-shaped hats by cutting halfway through paper plates, rolling them into cone shapes and taping along the cut edges.

Extension: Help the children put on their decorated hats. Then play music and let them march around the room in a Hat Parade.

It's Hat Weather

Sung to: "London Bridge"

When the wind blows all around,
All around, all around,
When the wind blows all around,
It's hat weather!

When the rain comes pouring down,
Pouring down, pouring down,
When the rain comes pouring down,
It's hat weather!

When the snow is on the ground,
On the ground, on the ground,
When the snow is on the ground,
It's hat weather!

Elizabeth McKinnon

Snacks in a Hat

Partially fill recloseable plastic sandwich bags with snack foods such as dried fruit bits, raisins, nuts and pretzels. Seal the bags and place them in a large hat. Then pass the hat around and let each child reach in and take out a snack.

Variation: Decorate a large coffee can or an ice-cream bucket to resemble a hat and place the snacks inside.

What Can You Be?

Set out a number of different kinds of hats. Include dress-up hats and hats from various occupations such as firefighter, police officer and cowhand. Then let the children take turns selecting a hat to wear as you sing the following song:

Sung to: "Row, Row, Row Your Boat"

What, what can you be
With a hat like that?
You can be a _____ ,
With a hat like that.

Cindy Dingwall
Palatine, IL

Sun Day

In parts of Norway there is no sunlight at all in the middle of winter. When the sun begins to appear again around the end of January, the children get to celebrate *Soldag,* or Sun Day, by staying home from school and playing outside. Plan to have your celebration the first day the sun comes out after a long gray spell. Besides doing the activities below, you might wish to let the children enjoy the outdoor sunshine by playing a game of shadow tag.

Sun Day Beach Picnic

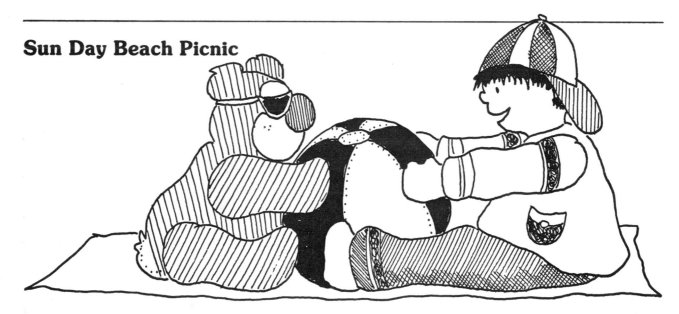

In honor of Sun Day, let the children have an indoor "beach picnic" at snacktime. Spread a blanket or a tablecloth on the floor and add some shells, a beach ball or a beach umbrella for decorations. Serve yellow foods such as deviled eggs, unpeeled banana sections or pineapple chunks.

Extension: For added fun, make sunglasses for the children to wear while they enjoy their picnic. Cut eyeglass shapes out of posterboard and glue colored cellophane squares over the eyeholes. Then attach pipe cleaners to the sides of the frames and bend them to fit over the children's ears.

Winter Sun

Recite the poem below and let the children fill in the blanks.

Winter sun, don't you run,
Stay with me and have some fun.
Shine on the _____ , shine on me,
Shine on the _____ , shine on the tree.
Shine on the _____ , shine so fair,
Shine on the _____ , shine everywhere!

Jean Warren

Paper Plate Suns

Cut 1- by 2-inch rectangles out of yellow crepe paper or tissue paper. Let the children paint paper plates yellow. While the paint is still wet, have them press the paper rectangles all over the centers of their plates as well as around the edges to create sun rays. (If the paint dries before the children have finished, let them use glue.) Then hang the suns from the ceiling or on a wall to give your room a bright sunshiny look.

Hello, Mr. Sun

Sung to: "If You're Happy and You Know It"

Hello, Mr. Sun, how are you?
    (Clap, clap.)
Hello, Mr. Sun, how are you?
    (Clap clap.)
We're so glad you're out today,
And we hope that you will stay.
We just love to see you shine, yes, we do!
    (Clap, clap.)

Elizabeth McKinnon

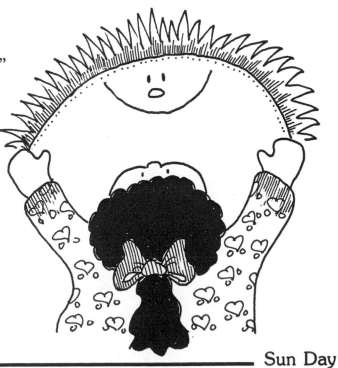

Sun Day

Groundhog Day

Groundhog Day is February 2. According to folklore, the groundhog comes up out of his winter burrow on this day. If it is sunny and the groundhog sees his shadow, he will go back into his burrow to sleep, which means that there will be six more weeks of winter. If the day is cloudy and the groundhog cannot see his shadow, he will remain outside, indicating that spring will soon arrive.

Groundhog Puppets

Cut groundhog faces (about 1½ inches in diameter) out of brown construction paper. Let the children brush glue on their shapes and press on thin wisps of cotton for fur. Then let them glue on eye and nose shapes cut out of black construction paper. When they have finished, attach their groundhog faces to the tops of Popsicle sticks. Give each child a small paper cup with a slit cut in the bottom. Have the children push the bottoms of their Popsicle sticks down through the slits in their cups. Then show them how to move their Popsicle sticks up and down to make their groundhogs appear and disappear.

Groundhog, Groundhog

Let the children take turns popping up out of a cardboard carton "burrow" as everyone recites the poem below.

Groundhog, Groundhog, popping up today.
Groundhog, Groundhog, can you play?
If you see your shadow, hide away.
If there is no shadow, you can stay.
Groundhog, Groundhog, popping up today.
Groundhog, Groundhog, can you play?

Jean Warren

Hint: If desired, arrange your room so that you can create or take away a shadow. Overhead lights would eliminate a shadow and a low light aimed directly at the "groundhog" would create a shadow.

Groundhog Lunches

Groundhogs like to nibble on grasses and other greens that grow near their burrows. For "groundhog lunches," let the children help make watercress and romaine lettuce salads to eat with a favorite dressing.

Here's a Little Groundhog

Sung to: "I'm a Little Teapot"

Here's a little groundhog, furry and brown,
He's popping up to look around.
If he sees his shadow, down he'll go,
Then six more weeks of winter — oh, no!

Let the children use their groundhog puppets from the activity on the previous page to act out the movements described in the song.

Nancy Nason Biddinger
Orlando, FL

Abraham Lincoln's Birthday

Abraham Lincoln was born on February 12, 1809, in a humble log cabin. His family was very poor, so he couldn't always go to school. But by teaching himself and working hard, he rose to become our country's sixteenth President. Abraham Lincoln believed that all people should have equal rights, and today he is remembered as the President who gave the slaves their freedom. To add to your celebration, you might wish to let the children use Lincoln pennies to make coin rubbings.

Lincoln Penny Count

Number five index cards from 1 to 5. Give each child a paper cup "bank" containing five pennies. Have the children sit on the floor in a circle. Place a numbered index card in the center of the circle. Then have the children each count out on the floor the same number of pennies as the number on the card. Have them put their pennies back into their banks before you place another numbered card in the center of the circle. Continue the game until all the cards have been played.

Extension: Let the children take turns tossing pennies into an oatmeal box decorated to resemble a black top hat. Then remove the pennies and count them with the children.

Lincoln's Birthday Song

Sung to: "The Muffin Man"

Do you know whose birthday's today,
Birthday's today, birthday's today?
Do you know whose birthday's today?
It's Abraham Lincoln's.

He wanted all people to be free,
To be free, to be free.
He wanted all people to be free.
Let's honor him today.

Jean Warren

Log Cabin Mural

Lay brown paper lunch bags out flat and cut off the bottom flaps. Roll up each bag lengthwise and tape along the edges to make "logs." Place a sheet of butcher paper on a table or on the floor. Then let the children work together to glue the logs on the butcher paper in a log cabin shape. When they have finished, add a construction paper chimney and several green tree shapes, if desired. Display the mural on a wall or a bulletin board.

Variation: Use any size of brown paper bags to make the logs and cut them to a uniform length.

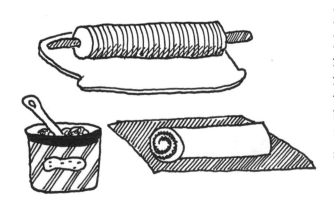

Lincoln Log Sandwiches

Let the children make "Lincoln log sandwiches" for snacktime. Have them use a rolling pin to flatten slices of whole-wheat bread. Then have them spread on peanut butter and roll up their bread slices to create "logs." Let the children sing "Happy Birthday" to Abe before enjoying their snacks.

Abraham Lincoln's Birthday

Heart Day

February is the time for hearts — Valentine hearts and human hearts. By celebrating Heart Day during American Heart Month in February, you can help the children begin to learn about their own hearts and how they work. Besides doing the activities below, you might wish to show pictures from library books of the human heart and circulatory system.

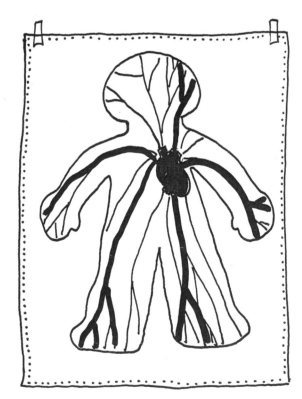

How the Heart Works

Explain to the children that the heart is a muscle inside the chest that is about the size of a fist. As the heart beats, it pumps blood to all parts of the body through tubes called "arteries" and "veins." Give each child a large precut paper doll with a red heart drawn on the left side of its chest. Let the children use red crayons to draw lines on their paper dolls showing how the heart pumps blood out through the arteries to different parts of the body. Then have them use blue crayons to draw lines showing how that blood travels back to the heart through the veins.

Listen to the Heartbeats

Bring in a stethoscope and let the children use it to listen to one another's hearts. Ask them to try describing the sound that the heart makes as it beats ("lub-*dub*, lub-*dub*"). Let them listen to one another's hearts while sitting quietly, then after doing jumping jacks. What differences can they hear in the heartbeats? Talk about how our hearts need both rest and exercise in order to stay healthy and strong.

Heartbeats

Sung to: "The Farmer in the Dell"

Lub-*dub*, lub-*dub*, lub-*dub*,
　(Sing slowly.)
Lub-*dub*, lub-*dub*, lub-*dub*.
When I (rest / sleep / etc.) my heart beats slow,
Lub-*dub*, lub-*dub*, lub-*dub*.

Lub-*dub*, lub-*dub*, lub-*dub*,
　(Sing fast.)
Lub-*dub*, lub-*dub*, lub-*dub*.
When I (run/jump/etc.) my heart beats fast,
Lub-*dub*, lub-*dub*, lub-*dub*.

Elizabeth McKinnon

Happy Heart Salads

Fish, fruits and vegetables are among the foods that are good for our hearts. Let the children help prepare the following salad ingredients. flaked tuna, diced apples and celery, shredded carrots, raisins, plain lowfat yogurt (for dressing). Then let them mix spoonfuls of the different ingredients together in small bowls to make "happy heart salads."

George Washington's Birthday

February 22 is the birthday of George Washington, the man we call the "Father of Our Country." Washington was born in 1732 and grew up to become a famous general. Later, he helped form our nation's government and was elected to be our first President. As part of your Washington's Birthday celebration, read or tell the story about young George and the cherry tree.

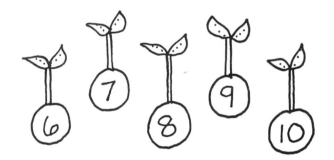

Washington Cherry Count

Make a felt tree and ten felt cherries and place the tree on a flannelboard. Use a felt-tip marker to number the cherries from 1 to 10. Let each child in turn choose a cherry, identify the number on it and place the cherry on the tree. When all the cherries are on the tree, count them together with the children.

Washington's Birthday Placemats

Glue Washington quarters along the short edges of an 8½- by 11-inch piece of cardboard. When the glue has dried, let the children place sheets of typing paper on top of the cardboard and rub across the quarters with black crayons. Then let them glue circles punched out of red construction paper with a hole punch on the centers of their papers for cherries. If desired, cover the placemats with clear self- stick paper.

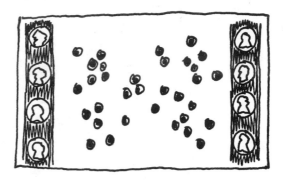

Washington's Birthday Song

Sung to: "The Muffin Man"

Do you know whose birthday's today,
Birthday's today, birthday's today?
Do you know whose birthday's today?
It's George Washington's.

He was America's first President,
First President, first President.
He was America's first President.
Let's honor him today.

Jean Warren

Washington's Birthday Snacks

At snacktime spoon cherry yogurt into small bowls. Then let each child top his or her serving with a sprinkling of nut-like cereal and a red cherry. Before enjoying their snacks, let the children sing "Happy Birthday" to George.

George Washington's Birthday

Carnival

In many places throughout the world, the days leading up to Ash Wednesday are a time of feasting and merrymaking called Carnival. This holiday originated as a last means of having fun before the 40-day Lenten season of fasting began. Today, Carnival is celebrated with singing and dancing, lavish costume parades, masked balls and elaborate pageants. To make your Carnival day special, you might wish to decorate your room with crepe paper streamers and invite the children to come dressed in costumes.

Carnival Masks

Make a mask for each child by cutting eye, nose and mouth holes out of a paper plate. Let the children decorate their masks with felt-tip markers. Then let them glue on materials such as colored paper scraps, yarn, sequins and glitter. When the glue has dried, attach the bottom part of each mask to a paper headband that fits around the child's forehead, making sure that the chin of the mask is above the child's eyes. (Masks worn this way will not interfere with the children's seeing or breathing.)

Extension: Let the children show off their masks by taking part in a Carnival Parade. If they are not wearing costumes, tie colorful crepe paper streamers around their waists. Then play music and let them have fun parading and dancing around the room.

Carnival Cookies

In separate bowls mix white frosting with drops of different colored food coloring to create bright shades. Give each child a large flat cookie, a Popsicle stick and a paper plate containing small spoonfuls of the different colored frosting. Let the children use their Popsicle sticks to spread the frosting on their cookies. Then pass around cookie sprinkles, shredded coconut and raisins and let the children decorate their cookies any way they wish.

Variation: For a sugarless alternative, tint soft cream cheese with food coloring and let the children spread it on crackers. Then let them add raisins, nuts and dried fruit bits for decorations.

Carnival Time Is Here

Sung to: "The Mulberry Bush"

Let's clap and sing for Carnival,
 (Clap hands.)
Carnival, Carnival.
Let's clap and sing for Carnival,
Carnival time is here.

Let's dance and sing for Carnival,
 (Dance in place.)
Carnival, Carnival.
Let's dance and sing for Carnival,
Carnival time is here.

Let's twirl and sing for Carnival,
 (Twirl around.)
Carnival, Carnival.
Let's twirl and sing for Carnival,
Carnival time is here.

Additional verses: "Let's skip and sing for Carnival; Let's hop and sing for Carnival."

Elizabeth McKinnon

Matching Masks

Use small paper plates (or construction paper circles) to make five different pairs of matching masks. Attach Popsicle stick handles, if desired. Mix up the masks and place them in a pile. Then let the children have fun finding the matching pairs of masks and holding them up to their faces.

Carnival

Pancake Day

In England making and eating pancakes is traditional on Shrove Tuesday, or Pancake Day. The custom dates back to times when people were not allowed to eat eggs and butter during Lent, so they used up their leftovers by making pancakes the day before Lent began. One of the best-known Pancake Day celebrations takes place each year in the town of Olney. The highlight of the celebration is a pancake race in which women flip pancakes in pans as they run.

Pancake Games

Cut 3-inch "pancakes" out of a brown cardboard carton and let the children use them to play the games below.

Pancake Toss — Hold a pie pan containing a pancake with both hands. Toss up the pancake and try catching it in the pan.

Pancake Walk — Walk across the room and back while balancing a pancake on a pancake turner.

Pancake Drop — Stand beside a large frying pan placed on the floor and drop in a designated number of pancakes.

Pancake Match — Use a pancake turner to flip over pancakes that have been marked with colors or numbers to find matching pairs.

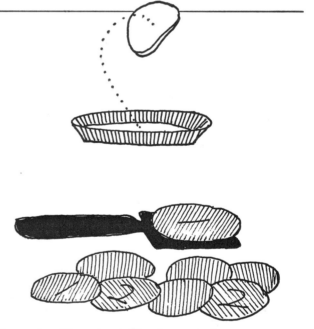

Pancake Count — Stack pancakes on paper plates and count the number of pancakes in each stack.

Pancake Man Finger Puppets

Cut 5-inch circles out of large white index cards and make two finger holes near the bottom of each circle. Have the children color their circles with brown crayons to make "pancakes." Let them glue on precut construction paper eye and mouth shapes. Then show them how to stick two of their fingers through the holes in their puppets to make legs.

Extension: Read or tell the story of the Pancake Man and let the children use their puppets to act out the movements. Or let them make up their own stories to act out with their Pancake Man puppets.

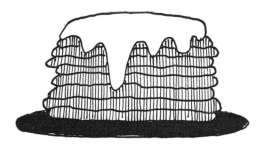

Cooking Up Pancakes

Sung to: "Skip to My Lou"

Cooking up pancakes, one by one,
Cooking up pancakes, one by one,
Cooking up pancakes, one by one.
Put 'em on a platter when they are done.

Serving up pancakes, two by two,
Serving up pancakes, two by two,
Serving up pancakes, two by two.
Some for me and some for you.

Pouring on syrup, oh, so sweet,
Pouring on syrup, oh, so sweet,
Pouring on syrup, oh, so sweet.
Come on, everyone, let's all eat!

Elizabeth McKinnon

Pancakes

Make pancakes using a favorite recipe. Or mix together 2 cups flour and a pinch of salt. Add 2 well-beaten eggs and just enough milk to make a thin batter. Drop the batter by spoonfuls into a hot greased skillet and cook until golden brown on both sides. Serve warm with butter and Strawberry Syrup (recipe follows).

Strawberry Syrup — In a blender combine 1 cup strawberries with ¼ cup unsweetened frozen apple juice concentrate. Process until smooth.

Pig Day

Pig lovers are in hog heaven on March 1, for that is National Pig Day. To celebrate, they hold neighborhood pig parties where they enjoy "pig-out" feasts and exchange pig presents. They also use the day to promote appreciation of pigs for being the intelligent, clean animals they truly are. Despite what most people think, pigs don't spend their days wallowing in mud; they burrow in it only when they have no other means of keeping cool. As part of your Pig Day celebration, let the children recite the nursery rhymes "This Little Piggy Went to Market" and "To Market, to Market, to Buy a Fat Pig."

Pig Puppets

Let the children paint paper plates light pink to use for pig faces. Cut ear shapes and circles for noses out of a darker shade of pink construction paper (or use pink felt, wallpaper, foil or fabric). When the plates have dried, let the children glue on the ear and nose shapes. Have them each glue two circles punched out of black construction paper with a hole punch on their pig noses for nostrils. Then let them glue on larger black circles for eyes. Attach Popsicle sticks to the backs of the pig faces for handles.

Extension: Read or tell the story of the Three Little Pigs and let the children act out the movements with their pig puppets.

Piglets

Have the children form a group and pretend to be piglets playing in a pigpen. Choose one child to be the Parent Pig. When the Parent Pig closes his or her eyes and "falls asleep," signal one of the piglets to run away and hide somewhere in the room. Then have the Parent Pig wake up and go searching for the missing piglet. As the Parent Pig walks around the room, have the piglets in the pigpen oink loudly if he or she is going in the right direction or oink softly if he or she is going in the wrong direction. When the missing piglet has been found and brought back to the pigpen, choose new players and start the game again.

Hint: Before playing the game, attach a piece of curled pink ribbon to the back of each child's waist for a "pig tail."

Pink Pig-Sicles

Mix together 2 cups plain yogurt, one 12-ounce can unsweetened frozen apple-cranberry juice concentrate and 2 teaspoons vanilla. Pour the mixture into small paper cups and insert plastic spoons for handles. Chill in the freezer until set, then serve as treats for snacktime. Makes 8 to 10 servings.

This Little Piggy

Sung to: "Frere Jacques"

This little piggy, this little piggy,
Went to town, went to town.
He ran up and down,
He ran up and down,
Through the town, through the town.

This little piggy, this little piggy,
He stayed home, he stayed home.
He didn't like to roam,
He didn't like to roam.
He stayed home, he stayed home.

Jean Warren

Peanut Day

March is National Peanut Month, a time to honor the peanut and its most popular product, peanut butter. Choose any day during March to celebrate. Besides doing the activities below, you might wish to plan a few peanut games. For example, have a Peanut Toss or a Peanut Hunt. Or have a Peanut Race and let the children push peanuts across the floor with their noses. Follow up by providing handfuls of peanuts for counting, shelling and tasting.

Peanut Shell Collages

Use this activity to recycle the peanut shells saved from other activities in this unit. Cut peanut shapes out of heavy brown paper bags or brown construction paper. Pour glue into shallow containers and set out bowls of peanut shells. Then let the children dip the shells (rounded sides up) into the glue and place them all over their peanut shapes.

The Peanut Plant

Explain that although we think of peanuts as nuts, they really belong to the same family as peas and beans. Then use the following poem to help the children understand how peanuts grow.

Up through the ground the peanut plant grows,
(Crouch down near floor.)

Peeking out its little green nose.
(Slowly start to rise.)

Reaching, reaching for the sky,
(Raise arms above head.)

Growing, growing, growing high.
(Stand on tiptoe.)

Then the flower starts to grow,
(Make circle with arms.)

But it doesn't grow up! Not it! Oh, no!
(Shake head.)

Down it goes, sending shoots underground,
(Bend over and touch floor with fingers.)

And there grow the peanuts, plump and round!
(Kneel and pretend to dig up peanuts.)

Author Unknown

Homemade Peanut Butter

Let the children help shell a package of unsalted roasted peanuts. Then have them grind the peanuts in a food grinder. Mix the ground nuts with ¼ cup softened margarine and add salt to taste. Serve on crackers, apple slices or celery sticks. Or, for a special treat, spread on slices of whole-wheat toast and top with warm applesauce.

Variation: Make peanut butter in a blender, using 1 to 3 tablespoons vegetable oil for each cup peanuts.

Peanut Butter

Sung to: "Frere Jacques"

Peanut butter, peanut butter,
Good for you, fun to chew.
Put peanuts in a blender,
Add a little oil.
Let it whirl, let it swirl.

Peanut butter, peanut butter,
Now it's done; oh, what fun!
Spread it on a sandwich,
Spread it on a cracker.
Good for you, fun to chew.

Susan Peters
Upland, CA

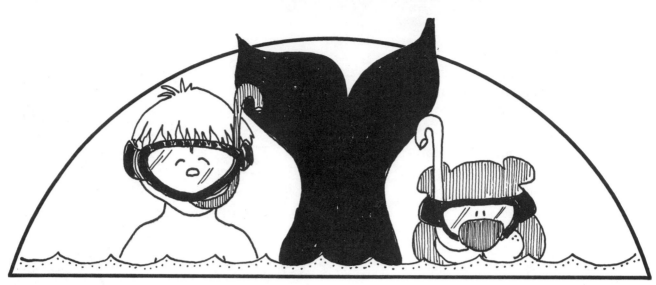

Whale Festival

In mid-March several towns along the California coast celebrate the whale-watching season with Whale Festivals. Among the highlights of the festivals are special whale-watching tours and cruises. California gray whales spend their summers feeding in the Bering Sea and Arctic Ocean. They migrate 4,000 miles to the warm waters off Mexico and Southern California to winter and give birth to their babies. Then they start back up the coast again in early spring, which is the best time to catch sight of them. Choose any day in March to have your whale celebration. Besides doing the activities below, show pictures of whales and point out that their noses, or blowholes, are located on the tops of their heads. Explain that when whales rise to the ocean's surface, they breathe out through their blowholes, sending spouts of water high up into the air.

Stuffed Whales

For each child cut two large whale shapes out of butcher paper. Put the two shapes together and staple around the edges, leaving an opening on one side. Let the children stuff their whales with squares of crumpled newspaper. Then staple the openings closed. Set out gray, black and white tempera paints and let the children paint their whales any way they wish. When the paint has dried, attach pieces of yarn to the tops of the whales for handles. Or turn your room into an "ocean" by hanging the whales from the ceiling.

Extension: If desired, let the children also make baby whales. Then attach the babies to the undersides of the mothers.

Five Big Whales

Cut five whale shapes out of gray or black felt and five spout shapes out of white felt. Lay a piece of blue yarn across a flannelboard to represent the surface of the sea and place the whale shapes beneath it. Then recite the poem below and let the children take turns moving the whale shapes up to the water's surface and placing the spout shapes above the whales' heads.

Five big whales in the sea offshore,
One swam up to spout, and that left four.
Four big whales in the deep blue sea,
One swam up to spout, and that left three.
Three big whales in the sea so blue,
One swam up to spout, and that left two.
Two big whales having lots of fun,
One swam up to spout, and that left one.
One big whale longing for the sun,
It swam up to spout, and that left none.

Elizabeth McKinnon

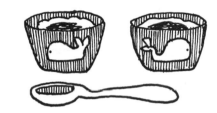

Whales-in-the-Sea

For snacktime make lime gelatin and spoon it into small paper cups. Then give each child a dried prune "whale" to place in his or her green gelatin "sea."

I'm a Great Big Whale

Sung to: "I'm a Little Teapot"

I'm a great big whale,
Watch me swim.
Here is my blowhole,
   (Point to back of head.)
Here are my fins.
   (Wave hands against body.)
See me flip my tail as down I go,
   (Pretend to dive.)
Then up I come and "Whoosh!" I blow.
   (Raise arms above head to form spout.)

Elizabeth McKinnon

Nutrition Day

March is National Nutrition Month, so choose any day to celebrate. Use this opportunity to introduce the children to the four major food groups — milk and dairy products, fruits and vegetables, breads and grains, and meats and other proteins. Talk with the children about how our bodies need foods from each of these groups every day in order to grow and stay strong and healthy.

Paper Plate Meals

Have the children look through magazines to find pictures of different kinds of foods. Then have them tear or cut out the pictures and glue them on paper plates to make "breakfasts," "lunches" or "dinners." While they are working, talk about the importance of eating balanced meals and encourage them to choose pictures of nutritious foods from the four major food groups when putting their meals together.

Nutritious Snacks

Set out foods from the four major food groups, such as cheese cubes or cottage cheese, apple slices or carrot sticks, bread triangles or crackers and deviled ham or tuna salad. Then give each child a plate and let him or her choose one food from each of the four groups to eat for snacks.

Extension: Discuss the importance of choosing nutritious snacks over snacks that contain a lot of added sugar. Label one shoebox with a "happy face" and another with a "sad face." Then help the children sort magazine pictures of nutritious snack foods and sugary snack foods into the appropriate boxes.

They're So Good for You

Sung to: "Row, Row, Row Your Boat"

Milk, fruits and vegetables,
Meat and bread, too.
Try to have some every day,
They're so good for you!

Elizabeth McKinnon

Shopping Game

Cut out magazine pictures of nutritious foods from the four major food groups. For example: milk, cheese, yogurt, cottage cheese; apples, oranges, peas, potatoes; bread, cereal, crackers, pasta; meat, chicken, fish, eggs. Cover the pictures with clear self-stick paper for durability. Have the children sit in a circle and help divide the pictures into four groups. Then let one child at a time "go shopping" by choosing a picture from each group and placing it in a small shopping basket. Have the child name the foods. Then let the next child replace the pictures in the proper groups and choose four pictures of his or her own to place in the basket. Continue the game until everyone has had a turn.

Variation: Use real foods or empty food containers instead of pictures.

April Fool's Day

April Fool's Day on April 1 is a favorite day for playing tricks. As part of the fun, have the children wear their shirts or sweaters backward and greet each other by saying "goodbye" instead of "hello." Or rearrange your room by turning objects upside down or backward and let the children name all the things that are different.

Silly Mixed-Up Creatures

Cut pictures of people and animals out of magazines. Then cut the pictures in half to make "tops" and "bottoms." Place all the tops in one pile and all the bottoms in another. Provide the children with construction paper and glue. Then let them choose tops and bottoms to put together and glue on their papers to create "silly mixed-up creatures."

Variation: Let the children erase the faces on magazine pictures of people or animals. Then have them use felt-tip markers to draw on funny faces of their own.

April Fool Rhymes

Recite the poem below, each time substituting a new third line and letting the children name a rhyming word at the end. For example: "I saw a cat who was wearing a hat; I saw a fish who was washing a dish; I saw a bear who was combing its hair." When the children become familiar with the poem, encourage them to make up their own April Fool rhymes.

I saw a sight today,

While on my way to school.

I saw a bee with a shoe on its knee.

Surprise! April Fool!

Elizabeth McKinnon

Variation: Sing the words of the poem to the tune of "The Farmer in the Dell."

Turn-About Snacktime

When it's time for snacks, let the children walk backward to the snack table. Start with dessert first. Then serve crackers and cheese and let the children make inside-out sandwiches (instead of placing cheese between two crackers, have them each put a cracker between two slices of cheese). For added fun, pour juice from a well-scrubbed flower vase or coffee pot.

Giant, Giant Spider

Sung to: "Eensy, Weensy Spider"

Giant, giant spider,

Crawling up your back.

Here, let me help you

Give your back a whack.

It was very ugly,

So very mean and cruel.

Aren't you glad I saved you?

Happy April Fool!

Jean Warren

Cherry Blossom Festival

Washington, D.C. is famous for its thousands of cherry trees, originally given to our country by Japan as a memorial of friendship. In early April when the trees are in full bloom, visitors come from all over to take part in the annual Cherry Blossom Festival. Highlights include a huge parade with marching bands and floats, musical concerts and plenty of opportunities for viewing the clouds of pink and white cherry blossoms. To make your celebration special, plan to have it on a day when the flowering trees in your area are in bloom.

Blossoming Cherry Trees

For each child use a brown crayon to draw a picture of a bare tree on a sheet of light blue construction paper. Pour glue into shallow containers. Let the children shake popped popcorn in paper lunch bags with a mixture of baby powder and red powder tempera paint. Then have them dip the pink popcorn "blossoms" into the glue and place them on their bare tree pictures to create flowering cherry trees. When the glue has dried, display the pictures on a wall or a bulletin board.

Variation: Instead of using popcorn, let the children make blossoms by twisting 2-inch squares of pink tissue paper around pencil erasers.

Cherry Blossoms

Sung to: "Eensy, Weensy Spider"

Little cherry blossom buds,
Closed up oh, so tight.
>(Lower head and hug self.)

See them bursting into bloom,
Colored pink and white.
>(Raise head and open arms wide.)

Along comes the spring breeze,
Blowing all around,
>(Wave arms gently.)

And down fall the petals,
Twirling to the ground.
>(Flutter fingers downward in circles.)

Elizabeth McKinnon

Cherry Blossom Fun

If you have flowering cherry trees in your area, take the children on a walk to see the blossoms. Encourage them to tell what they think the blossoms look like (pink clouds, pink snowflakes, etc.). If desired, write down their responses to keep for reading and illustrating later.

Variation: Plan a Cherry Blossom Parade for indoor fun. Let the children make floats by decorating cardboard boxes with pink paper blossoms and crepe paper streamers. Add twine or yarn handles. Then let the children place stuffed animals in their floats and pull them around the room while you play music.

Cherry Blossom Snacks

Make or purchase small round sugar cookies. Let the children frost the cookies with pink icing and sprinkle on shredded coconut to make "cherry blossoms."

Variation: For a sugarless alternative, mix soft cream cheese with drops of red food coloring. Let the children spread the pink cheese on round crackers. Then have them sprinkle on unsweetened shredded coconut (available at health food stores).

Cherry Blossom Festival

Arbor Day

Arbor Day is the time for planting new trees in yards, public parks, neighborhoods and communities. National Arbor Day is celebrated on the last Friday in April, but the date of each state's Arbor Day varies depending upon the growing season. Arbor Day is also a time to appreciate trees both for their beauty and for their usefulness. Talk with the children about how trees provide us with shade, food and firewood as well as wood for making such things as paper, houses and furniture.

Four Seasons Trees

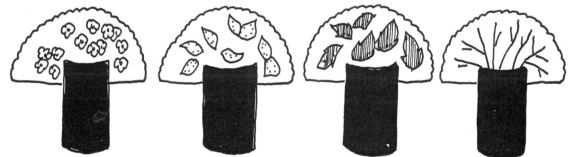

Let the children make trees for each of the four seasons. For each child you will need four cardboard toilet tissue tubes and two paper plates. Cut two slits directly opposite each other in one end of each toilet tissue tube. Cut the paper plates in half. Have the children paint their toilet tissue tubes brown to make trunks. Then have them use crayons or felt-tip markers to decorate one of their paper plate halves with blossoms, one with green leaves, one with red and orange leaves and one with bare tree branches. When they have finished, help them insert their paper plate halves in the slits in their brown cardboard tubes to complete their trees.

Extension: For a sequencing game, let the children try lining up their trees in the order of the seasons, starting with a different season each time.

Hug a Tree Today

Read the poem below to the children. Then take them on a walk to look for special trees to hug. Along the way, have them compare such things as tree shapes and sizes, kinds and shapes of foliage and types of bark.

Why not hug a tree today
Or pat it on its bark?
Give a tree a great big squeeze
At home or in the park.

Find the tree you like the best
And stand beneath its shade.
Stretch your arms around its trunk
And hug until you fade.

Imagine the birds that have lived in your tree,
Imagine the squirrel in its nest.
A tree is a home to all that come,
The perfect place to rest.

So put your arms around your tree,
Whether it's short or tall.
Hug your tree — you'll feel so good,
Winter, spring, summer or fall.

Susan M. Paprocki
Northbrook, IL

Tree Treats

At snacktime let the children taste a variety of foods that grow on trees. For example: fruits such as apples, pears, bananas and oranges; nuts such as walnuts, hazelnuts and pecans; olives; chocolate or cocoa (which are made from the seeds of the cacao tree).

Extension: Let the children help plant tree seeds for Arbor Day. Remove the seeds from an orange (or a grapefruit or lemon) and immediately plant them about ½ inch down in a pot of soil. Water well, then cover the pot with clear plastic and place it in a sunny spot. The seeds will germinate in three to four weeks, and soon small plants will appear. Remove the plastic when the plants are a few inches tall.

It's Arbor Day Today

Sung to: "The Farmer in the Dell"

It's Arbor Day today,
We're planting our trees this way.
   (Make planting movements.)
Matthew is planting an apple tree
For Arbor Day today.

Let the children name the kinds of trees they would like to plant for Arbor Day. Then sing a verse of the song for each child.

Elizabeth McKinnon

Arbor Day

Litterbag Day

April is Keep America Beautiful Month, and the last Friday is traditionally celebrated as National Litterbag Day. Throughout the month volunteers work together to clean up their neighborhoods and communities, and on Litterbag Day they distribute free litterbags to educate people about ways of handling trash. For your celebration, you might want to adopt the slogan "Don't Be a Litterbug — Use a Litterbag."

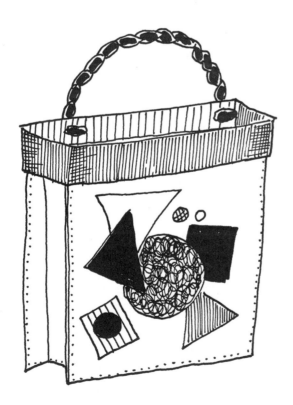

Litterbags

Let the children make litterbags to hang in their rooms at home or to give as gifts for use in their families' cars. Give each child a paper lunch bag. Cut different colors of construction paper into circles, squares and triangles and let the children glue the shapes on their bags. For each child cut a band of construction paper (1½ inches wide) to fit around the top edge of his or her bag. Help the children glue on their bands, which will allow the bags to remain open. Punch two holes (about 3 inches apart) near the top of the back of each bag. Then insert and tie yarn to make hangers.

Trash Song

Sung to: "London Bridge"

Trash is blowing all around,
All around, all around.
Trash is blowing all around,
All around the town.

Let's get busy and pick it up,
Pick it up, pick it up.
Let's get busy and pick it up,
All around the town.

Put the trash in a big trash bag,
Big trash bag, big trash bag.
Put the trash in a big trash bag,
All around the town.

Carol Mellott
Superior, NE

Brown Bag Snacks

Wrap snacks such as crackers, cheese cubes and apple slices separately in plastic wrap or waxed paper. Place the snacks in brown paper lunch bags, adding paper napkins and small containers of juice, if desired. Let the children enjoy their "brown bag snacks" outdoors, if possible. When they have finished, provide a large trash bag and have them each take care of gathering up their empty bags and food wrappers and throwing them away. While they are working, let them sing the following song:

Sung to: "Frere Jacques"

We're not litterbugs,
We're not litterbugs,
No siree, no siree!
We pick up our trash,
We pick up our trash,
Yes siree, yes siree!

Elizabeth McKinnon

Cleanup Brigade

Take the children on a walk around your school or neighborhood to pick up litter. Bring along a large plastic bag for collecting the trash. While the children are working, talk about how we help make our world a nicer place for everyone to live when we throw our litter in a trash can instead of on the ground. When you return from your walk, give everyone a gold star sticker for helping to "Keep America Beautiful."

Extension: If you have a recycling program in your area, let the children help sort the litter you collected into separate containers for paper products, plastics, cans and bottles.

Smell the Breezes Day

Children in Egypt celebrate the beginning of spring on *Sham-el-Neseem,* or Smell the Breezes Day, a holiday that falls in April or early May. In the morning they get up early and put on their new spring clothes — brightly colored dresses for the girls and striped shirts or robes for the boys. Then they help pack up picnic breakfasts which always include eggs dyed in beautiful shades of red, gold, purple and green. After that, the children and their families go out to a park or to the countryside to have their picnics and to enjoy the fresh sweet smells of spring.

Painted Egg Shapes

Cut an egg shape for each child out of white construction paper. Pour small amounts of condensed milk into the cups of a muffin tin and add drops of food coloring to each cup. Let the children use cotton swabs to brush different colored stripes of the glossy milk "paint" across their egg shapes. Then have them hold up their shapes to let the colors run together. Allow several days for the shapes to dry. (Note: Although painting with condensed milk is expensive, the brilliant colors created make it worth doing at least once a year.)

Variation: Let the children decorate their egg shapes with crayons or felt-tip markers. If desired, attach loops of yarn to the shapes and let the children wear them as necklaces.

Smell the Breezes

Sung to: "Did You Ever See a Lassie?"

Let's go out and smell the breezes,
The breezes, the breezes,
Let's go out and smell the breezes
On this fine spring day.
Smell fresh air and flowers,
Smell grass and spring showers.
Let's go out and smell the breezes
On this fine spring day.

Repeat, letting the children name other things they can smell outdoors in the spring.

Elizabeth McKinnon

Nature Walk

Take the children out for a walk to enjoy the fresh smells of spring. Ask them to name the different things they can smell as they sniff the spring breezes — flowers, damp soil, grass, etc. If possible, gather fresh leaves and small sprigs of evergreens for the children to crush in their hands and sniff.

Spring Picnic

Let the children help make pita bread sandwiches for an indoor or outdoor picnic. Moisten canned tuna or chicken with a mixture of plain yogurt and mayonnaise. Then let the children spoon small amounts of the mixture into pita pockets and sprinkle on shredded lettuce. Serve with cucumber sticks and cherry tomatoes, if desired. You might also wish to include a few dyed hard-boiled eggs in your picnic lunch for the children to share.

May Day

May Day on May 1 celebrates the passage of winter and the arrival of spring. The holiday is believed to have originated in Roman times as a festival of flowers. Today, children celebrate by making May baskets to fill with flowers and give secretly to friends. A common custom is to hang a May basket on a friend's front door, ring the doorbell and then run away.

May Baskets

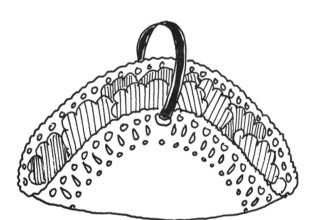

Give the children paper doilies to use for making simple May baskets. Cut small squares from a variety of colors of tissue paper. Let the children brush glue on the centers of their doilies. Then have them crumple the tissue paper squares and place them on top of the glue for flowers. Attach a ribbon or yarn handle to opposite sides of each doily. When the child holds onto the handle, the sides of the doily will curve up, turning the doily into a flower-filled "basket."

Variation: Let the children decorate margarine tubs, plastic berry baskets or cut-down milk cartons to make May baskets. Add pipe cleaner handles. Then let the children fill their baskets with real or paper flowers.

May Basket Game

Decorate an ordinary basket with ribbons or crepe paper streamers to make a May basket. Cut flower shapes out of different colors of construction paper and place them in a box. Have the children sit in a circle with the May basket in the center. Pass around the box of flowers and have each child choose one and name the color. Then sing the song below and let each child in turn skip around the inside of the circle and place his or her flower in the May basket.

Sung to: "A-Tisket, A-Tasket"

A-tisket, a-tasket,

A pretty May Day basket.

(Child's name) saw it on the porch

And put a (red/blue/etc.) flower in it.

Elizabeth McKinnon

When everyone has had a turn, put the flowers back into the box and start the game again, if desired.

May Day Snack Baskets

Let the children decorate Styrofoam cups with flower stickers or flower pictures cut from wrapping paper. Attach pipe cleaner handles to the cups to make baskets. At snacktime tuck a square of waxed paper inside each basket. Then add small pieces of fresh fruits for "flowers."

I'm a Little Basket

Sung to: "I'm a Little Teapot"

I'm a little basket,

Look at me —

Filled full of flowers,

Pretty as can be.

Hang me on a friend's door on May Day,

Then ring the bell and run away.

Elizabeth McKinnon

Pet Day

The first full week in May is the perfect time for honoring pets. Not only is it National Pet Week, it's Be Kind to Animals Week as well. Choose any day during the week for your celebration. Encourage the children to talk about their pets and discuss the things that pets need every day: food, water exercise, sleep and lots of loving attention. To help the children better understand how to care for pets, ask questions such as these: "If you were a kitten, how would you want someone to pet you? How would you want someone to pick you up? How would you feel if someone forgot to feed you?"

Pet Baskets

Give each child a small cardboard box and a pet animal shape cut from posterboard to fit inside the box. Set out materials such as construction paper scraps, felt-tip markers, animal stickers, cotton balls, fabric pieces and glue. Then let the children decorate their cardboard boxes and line them with soft materials to make sleeping baskets for their "pets." While they are working, encourage them to choose colors and materials they think their pets would especially like. When they have finished, let them place their pet shapes inside their decorated baskets.

Funny Animals

Place a stuffed animal for each child on the floor. Have the children sit in front of the animals in a semicircle. Let one child at a time walk around the animals as everyone recites the rhyme below. Then let the child choose any animal, take it back to the semicircle and give it a big kiss. Continue the game until everyone has had a turn.

One day while walking down the street,
Some funny animals I did meet.
One made a sound, just like this —
    (Child makes an animal sound.)
So I took it home and gave it a kiss.

Jean Warren

Love Your Pets

Sung to: "Row, Row, Row Your Boat"

Love, love, love your pets,
Love them every day.
Give them food and water, too.
Then let them run and play.

Love, love, love your pets,
Love them every night.
Let them sleep till they wake up,
In the morning light.

Elizabeth McKinnon

Animal Face Sandwiches

Let the children make "animal face sandwiches" for snacktime. Give them each a slice of whole-wheat toast and have them spread on peanut butter. Let them place raisins in the centers of their toast slices to make eyes and noses. Then give them thin slivers of pickles to add for whiskers and grated carrots to sprinkle on for fur.

Cinco de Mayo

Cinco de Mayo, or the Fifth of May, is one of Mexico's most important holidays. It commemorates the winning of a battle against the French on May 5, 1862, which eventually led to Mexican independence. Cinco de Mayo is celebrated in Mexico and in many Mexican-American communities with parades and marching bands and with fiestas that include music, dancing and feasting. In Mexico the celebrations end at night with displays of colorful fireworks.

Paper Flowers

Let the children make large flower decorations for your Cinco de Mayo celebration. Have them fingerpaint with bright colors on pieces of white butcher paper or construction paper. When the paint has dried, cut each paper into a large flower shape. Let the children make centers for their flowers by gluing on crumpled pieces of colored tissue paper. Then display the flowers on a wall or a bulletin board.

Variation: Use 6- by 12-inch rectangles cut from various colors of tissue paper to create tissue paper flowers. To make each flower, pinch the short edges of a rectangle together in the middle and place a 2-inch square of contrasting colored tissue paper on top. Twist the end of a pipe cleaner around the two pieces and fluff out the tissue to make petals.

Burritos

Let the children help make burritos for snacktime. Brown 1 pound ground beef and drain off the fat. Stir in one 16-ounce can refried beans and heat until warm. Place a small flour tortilla on each child's plate and top it with a few spoonfuls of the meat and bean mixture. Let the children sprinkle on grated cheese, if desired. Then roll up each tortilla and let the children enjoy eating their burritos with their fingers.

It's Cinco de Mayo Today

Sung to: "The Farmer in the Dell"

It's Cinco de Mayo today,
It's Cinco de Mayo today.
Let's clap our hands and shout "Olé!"
It's Cinco de Mayo today.

Additional verses: "Let's stomp our feet; Let's twirl around; Let's raise our arms; Let's circle round."

Elizabeth McKinnon

Cinco de Mayo Parade

Make your celebration come alive by playing library recordings of Mexican songs and letting the children march around the room in a Cinco de Mayo Parade. Tie brightly colored sashes of crepe paper around the children's waists and give them rhythm instruments to use for accompanying the music.

Variation: Instead of using ordinary rhythm instruments, make simple maracas for the children to shake by placing handfuls of dried beans or rice in paper lunch bags, folding down the tops and taping them closed. If desired, let the children decorate their maracas with strips of colored tissue paper or crepe paper.

Cinco de Mayo

Postcard Day

Plan to celebrate Postcard Day any time during National Postcard Week, which is the first full week in May. Picture postcards have been in use for about 100 years, and today many people collect them as a hobby. Some collectors commemorate National Postcard Week each year by designing special editions of their own postcards. To prepare for your celebration, you might wish to ask parents to donate used picture postcards. Or check for inexpensive cards at thrift stores or garage sales.

Postcard Games

Assemble a number of picture postcards to use for the games below.

- Let the children count the postcards.
- Have the children sort the postcards by categories (city scenes, landscape scenes, scenes that include people, scenes that include animals, etc.).
- Cut several postcards into puzzle pieces and let the children take turns putting them back together.
- Make numbered mailboxes out of shoeboxes and let the children "mail" the appropriate number of postcards in each box

- Place pairs of identical picture postcards in a pile and let the children find the matching pairs.

A Postcard, A Postcard

Sung to: "A-Tisket, A-Tasket"

A postcard, a postcard,
A pretty picture postcard,
I wrote a postcard to my friend,
And on the way I dropped it.
I dropped it, I dropped it,
And on the way I dropped it.
A little (boy/girl) picked it up
And put it in (his/her) pocket.

Have the children stand in a circle. As you sing the song, let one child skip around the outside of the circle, drop a postcard behind a second child, then join the circle again. Have the second child pick up the postcard and repeat the action as you sing the song again. Continue until everyone has had a turn.

Adapted Traditional

Designing Postcards

Let the children create their own postcards to give to family members or friends. Have them use crayons or felt-tip markers to draw pictures on 4- by 6-inch index cards. On the backs of the cards, write the children's dictated messages and the names of the intended recipients. Then let the children glue on small squares of colored paper for stamps.

Variation: Address each child's postcard to a person who lives in the child's home and let the children attach real postage stamps. Then take the children on a walk to mail their postcards in a nearby mailbox.

Postcard Toast

Cut the crusts off white bread slices. Pour milk into small bowls and add drops of different colored food coloring to each bowl. Let the children use new paint brushes to paint designs on their bread "postcards" with the colored milk. Then toast the bread and let the children brush on melted butter.

Postcard Day

Windmill Day

In Holland the second Saturday in May is National Windmill Day. On this day, many of the old windmills are put into operation for people to enjoy viewing. The windmills, which are now national monuments, were originally built to drain water from the land by pumping it into canals. Some of these historical windmills are still used today. As part of your celebration, you might wish to show pictures of windmills and talk about how they work.

Windmill Game

Choose one child to be the Leader and another child to be the Wind. Have the Leader walk around the room making windmill movements with his or her arms, swinging them first in one direction, then in another. Have the other children follow the Leader and copy his or her movements. When the Leader calls out "Windmill!" have everyone freeze in place. Then have the Wind move among the children, tapping each one on the shoulder. Once they have been tapped, have the children start swinging their arms around again. Then choose different children to be the Leader and the Wind for a new round of the game.

Windmills

Let the children paint cardboard toilet tissue tubes any color they wish to make windmill bases. Allow the paint to dry. To make windmill sails, cut index cards into 1- by 5-inch strips. Poke one hole in the middle of each sail and another hole about 1 inch from the top of each toilet tissue tube. Then attach two sails to each tube by inserting a brass paper fastener through all three holes. Let the children decorate the bases of their windmills by gluing on small construction paper tulip shapes.

Dutch Treats

Holland's dairy cows produce milk from which the well-known Edam and Gouda cheeses are made. Let the children sample these cheeses with crackers (or substitute other kinds of cheeses, if desired). Since chocolate is another famous Dutch product, you might wish to accompany your snack with cocoa.

I Wish I Were a Windmill

Sung to: "Did You Ever See a Lassie?"

Oh, I wish I were a windmill,
A windmill, a windmill.
Oh, I wish I were a windmill,
I know what I'd do.
I'd swing my arms this way,
I'd swing my arms that way.
Oh, I wish I were a windmill,
I know what I'd do.

Judith McNitt
Adrian, MI

Windmill Day

Mother's Day

Mother's Day is celebrated each year on the second Sunday in May. On this holiday people honor their mothers and thank them for all that they do by giving them tokens of appreciation such as cards, gifts and flowers. For your celebration, you can use the activities below or adapt the activities included in the Father's Day celebration on p. 114. (Note: Some children may wish to make Mother's Day cards or gifts for more than one person in their families.)

Fancy Soaps

Let the children make colored soaps to give as Mother's Day presents. Tint water with the desired color of food coloring and stir it into Ivory Snow to make a dough-like mixture (about 2 cups soap powder to ½ cup water). Have the children mold the mixture into balls or other shapes and place them on waxed paper to dry for several days. If the soaps are very small, let each child put several of them into a large baby food jar and decorate the lid with a sticker. Then tie a ribbon around the neck of each jar. Or help the children wrap their soaps in tissue paper and let them decorate their packages with stickers.

Variation: Give each of the children a long piece of thick yarn folded in half. Let each child use some of the soap mixture to form a ball around the folded end of his or her yarn piece.

Allow the soaps to dry on waxed paper. Then tie the loose ends of each child's yarn piece together to create a "soap-on-a-rope" for hanging over a shower head.

Spring

I Love Mommy

Sung to: "Frere Jacques"

I love Mommy, I love Mommy,
Yes, I do; yes, I do.
And my mommy loves me,
Yes, my mommy loves me,
Loves me, too; loves me, too.

Carla C. Skjong
Tyler, MN

Mother's Day Cards

Make cards by folding pieces of construction paper in half and writing "Happy Mother's Day" on the fronts. Talk with the children about the things that mothers do for their families. Then ask each child in turn to complete a sentence such as "My mom is special because _____," or "I love you, Mom, because _____," and write the sentence inside the child's card. Let the children decorate the fronts of their cards as desired. When they have finished, help them sign their names and write the date inside their cards.

Cookies for Mom

Use a favorite recipe to make sugar cookies. Let the children help roll out the dough and cut out shapes with cookie cutters. Bake according to your recipe directions. Set out frosting and cookie sprinkles. Then let each child decorate one cookie to give to Mom and one to eat for snacktime. Place each gift cookie in a plastic sandwich bag and attach a pretty ribbon bow.

Mother's Day

Lazybones Day

Children in Holland have special fun on *Luilak*, or Lazybones Day. Around four or five in the morning they gather in groups and walk through their towns making noise, singing songs and ringing doorbells to wake up all the "lazybones." Luilak originated as a celebration to trick winter into waking up and going away. Although the holiday traditionally takes place on the Saturday before Whitsunday, plan to have your celebration whenever winter is almost over in your area.

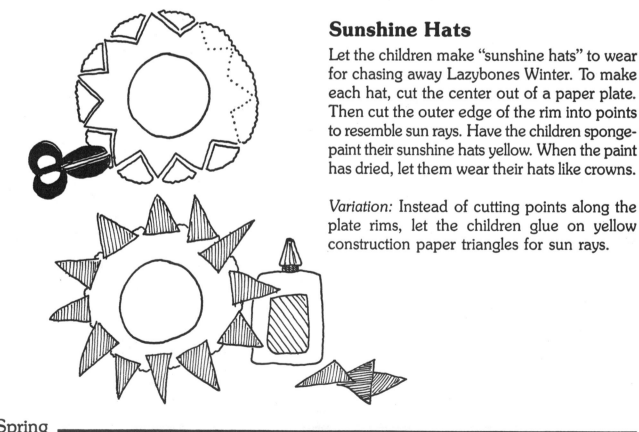

Sunshine Hats

Let the children make "sunshine hats" to wear for chasing away Lazybones Winter. To make each hat, cut the center out of a paper plate. Then cut the outer edge of the rim into points to resemble sun rays. Have the children sponge-paint their sunshine hats yellow. When the paint has dried, let them wear their hats like crowns.

Variation: Instead of cutting points along the plate rims, let the children glue on yellow construction paper triangles for sun rays.

Sunshine Shakes

"Sunshine shakes" make good wake-up drinks for lazybones. In a blender container place one 6-ounce can unsweetened frozen orange juice concentrate, ¾ cup milk, ¾ cup water, 1 teaspoon vanilla and 6 ice cubes. Blend until smooth and frothy, then pour into small cups. Makes 6 small servings.

Lazybones Winter, Will You Wake Up?

Sung to: "The Mulberry Bush"

Lazybones Winter, will you wake up,
Will you wake up, will you wake up?
Lazybones Winter, will you wake up?
Wake up and go away.

Lazybones Winter, you've stayed too long,
Stayed too long, stayed too long.
Lazybones Winter, you've stayed too long.
Wake up and go today.

Elizabeth McKinnon

Lazybones Wake-Up Parade

Give the children pan lids, wooden spoons and other loud rhythm instruments. Then take them outside and let them parade around, singing the song on this page and making noise to wake up old Lazybones Winter and make him go away. End the parade with one minute of extra-loud banging and shouting.

Dairy Day

Choose any day during June Dairy Month to say "thank you" to cows for all the good dairy products we enjoy. As part of your celebration, you might wish to display pictures of cows and talk about how cows are milked. You might also wish to let the children make a Dairy Mural by tearing pictures of dairy products out of magazines and gluing them on butcher paper. If possible, have them include pictures of milk, butter, cheese, cottage cheese, sour cream, ice cream, whipping cream and yogurt.

Ice-Cream Cones

For each child cut a large cone shape out of white construction paper and three circles out of colored construction paper. Have the children place their cone shapes on pieces of plastic screen (or any material that will make criss-cross impressions) and rub them with brown crayons. Then have each child glue his or her cone shape on a piece of paper and select three colored circles to glue on top to make a triple-decker ice-cream cone.

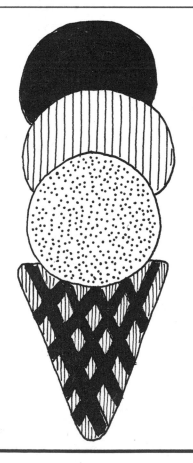

Variation: Mix evaporated milk with drops of food coloring in several small containers. Then let the children make "scoops of ice cream" to glue on top of their cones by painting white construction paper circles with the colored milk.

Making Butter

Fill baby food jars half full of whipping cream and screw the lids on tightly. Let two children take turns shaking each jar. After about six minutes the cream will be whipped, and after another minute or so, lumps of yellow butter will form. Rinse off the liquid whey and add a little salt, if desired, before spreading the butter on crackers for tasting.

Variation: Let the children observe as you use an electric mixer or an egg beater to whip the cream in a bowl. Stop for tasting. Then continue whipping the cream until butter forms.

Purple Cows

Make "purple cows" for the children to enjoy at snacktime. In a blender container place 1 cup milk, ¼ cup grape juice and 1 sliced banana. Blend until smooth and frothy, then pour into small cups. Makes 6 small servings.

Extension: For added fun, recite the following rhyme with the children:

I never saw a Purple Cow,
I never hope to see one.
But I can tell you, anyhow,
I'd rather see than be one!

Traditional

Thank You, Cows

Sung to: "Mary Had a Little Lamb"

Thank you, cows, for the milk we drink,
Milk we drink, milk we drink.
Thank you, cows, for the milk we drink.
We say "MOOO!" to you.

Additional verses: "Thank you, cows, for the butter on our bread; for the cheese on our crackers; for the cream on our pies; for cottage cheese and yogurt; for the ice cream we love."

Elizabeth McKinnon

Day of Swings

A favorite holiday in Korea is *Tano* Day, or the Day of Swings, which usually falls sometime in June. Every town celebrates by setting up a tall swing in a park and decorating it with festive red and white paper strips. In the morning the girls all dress in their best clothes and gather at the park for a swinging contest. Next to the swing is a tall pole with a little bell at the top. Whoever swings the highest and rings the bell most often wins a prize.

Tano Swing Fun

Take the children to a playground or a park that has swings. Decorate one of the swings by tying on red and white crepe paper streamers. Then give each child a few pushes in your Tano swing while everyone sings the song below. If desired, bring along a little bell to ring at the end of each child's turn.

Sung to: "Row, Row, Row Your Boat"

Pump, pump the Tano swing,
Pump it up so high.
You pump so high you touch the sky,
Then down you come again.

Jean Warren

Tano Day Fingerpainting

Red and white are the colors used in Korea for all festive occasions. To celebrate Tano Day, let the children fingerpaint red "swinging" designs on sheets of white butcher paper. Spray puffs of shaving cream in the centers of the papers and sprinkle on red powder tempera paint. Then have the children pretend that their hands are swings as they move them up and down and back and forth across their papers.

See Me Swinging

Sung to: "Frere Jacques"

See me swinging, see me swinging,
Oh, so high; oh, so high.
Higher and higher,
Higher and higher.
Touch the sky, touch the sky.

Saundra Winnett
Lewisville, TX

Gelatin Cotton Candy

Part of the fun on Tano Day is buying cotton candy and other sweets from vendors who walk through the holiday crowds. For your celebration, try making this sugarless "cotton candy" treat. Pour ¼ cup water into a bowl and add 2 envelopes unflavored gelatin. Stir and let sit for 5 minutes. Add ¾ cup boiling water and ¼ teaspoon red food coloring. Stir again until the gelatin is completely dissolved. Pour the mixture into a blender container and add one 6-ounce can unsweetened frozen apple juice concentrate. Blend until fluffy, then pour into paper cups. Chill for about 15 minutes.

Day of Swings

Father's Day

Father's Day is a special day for paying tribute to dads. The holiday is celebrated on the third Sunday in June by giving cards and gifts to express appreciation for fathers and for what they do. For your celebration, you can use the activities below or adapt the activities included in the Mother's Day celebration on p. 104. (Note: Some children may wish to make Father's Day cards or gifts for more than one person in their families.)

Father's Day Cards

Talk with the children about tasks they could do around the house to help their dads. Then let them make "helping hands" coupon booklets to give as Father's Day cards. Have them each make handprints on three or four sheets of paper. Staple each child's papers together with a cover on which you have written "Happy Father's Day." Then let the children decorate their covers as desired and help them sign their names. (Recipients of the cards can tear out the pages and present them to the children when they need helping hands.)

Snack Food Containers

Let the children make decorated snack food containers for Father's Day presents. Cut construction paper to fit around the sides of coffee cans (or other containers that have plastic lids). Have the children decorate their papers with crayons, felt-tip markers or paints. Then tape or glue the papers around the sides of the coffee cans and place a plastic lid on each can. If desired, let the children fill their containers with one of the snack foods suggested in the activity below.

Snacks for Dad

Let the children help make granola or popcorn to use for filling their decorated snack food containers. Or use the recipe below to make Nuts & Bolts. Be sure to make enough so that the children can enjoy some too.

Nuts & Bolts — Place 4 cups bite-sized shredded wheat in a baking pan in one layer. Sprinkle on ⅓ cup melted margarine and add a little garlic powder. Bake at 350 degrees for 15 minutes. When cool, stir in 1½ cups stick pretzels (broken in half), ½ cup raisins and ½ cup dry roasted peanuts. Makes about 6 cups.

Hint: If you have a large group, spoon the snacks into plastic sandwich bags and place one bag in each gift container.

Best Dad

Sung to: "This Old Man"

Father's Day, Father's Day
Is a very special day.
Here's a great big hug
And lots of kisses, too.
Each one says that I love you!

Susan Peters
Upland, CA

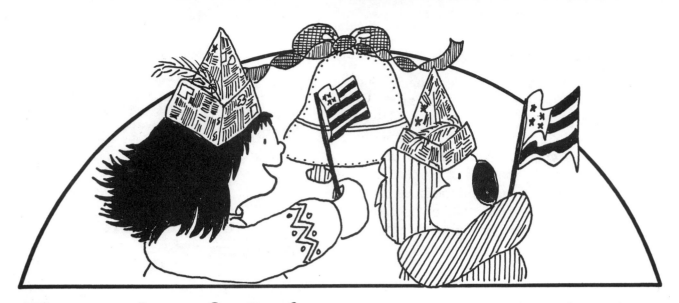

Fourth of July

The Fourth of July, or Independence Day, celebrates the signing of the Declaration of Independence in 1776. On July 4 we observe America's birthday by ringing bells, flying flags, joining in parades and setting off fireworks. As part of your celebration, you might wish to display an American flag and let the children count the stars and stripes. For added fun, hang a pretend Liberty Bell from the ceiling. Then let the children take turns tossing beanbags or rolled-up socks at the bell to make it ring.

Fireworks in the Sky

Sung to: "Row, Row, Row Your Boat"

Boom, crack, whistle, pop,
Fireworks in the sky.
See them lighting up the night
On the Fourth of July.

Red, blue, gold and green,
With fireworks we say,
"Happy Birthday, America,
It's Independence Day!"

Elizabeth McKinnon

Stars and Stripes Collages

Give each child a 9- by 12-inch sheet of blue construction paper. Cut a number of 1- by 9-inch "stripes" out of red and white construction paper. Set out glue and silver star stickers. Then let the children glue the stripes on their papers and attach the stars any way they wish to create their own "stars and stripes" designs.

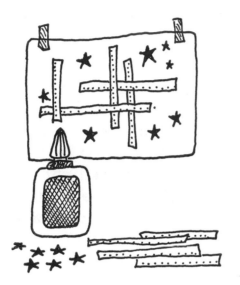

Fourth of July Sorting Game

Cut small, medium and large star shapes and Liberty Bell shapes out of red, white and blue construction paper. Mix up the shapes and place them in a pile. Then let the children take turns sorting the shapes according to color, shape or size.

Red, White and Blueberries

At snacktime place strawberries and blueberries in separate bowls. Let the children take turns mashing the berries with forks. Give each child some plain yogurt in a small bowl. Then let the children spoon both kinds of mashed berries over their yogurt to make Fourth of July treats. Before enjoying their snacks, let the children sing "Happy Birthday" to America.

Blueberry Day

Plan to celebrate Blueberry Day any time during "July Belongs to Blueberry Month." Fresh blueberries are plentiful during mid-summer, so have some available for the children to taste and examine. Talk about the color and shape of the berries and help the children discover the little "stars" on the ends. If you live in an area where blueberries grow, you might wish to take the children on a field trip to pick your own berries.

Blueberry Number Game

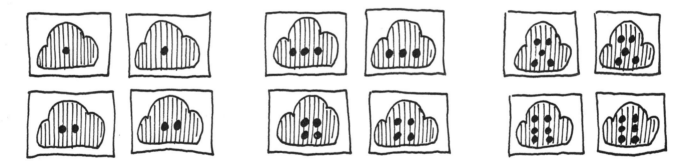

Cut twelve identical bush shapes out of green construction paper and glue each shape on a large index card. Divide the cards into six pairs. Then number the pairs of cards from 1 to 6 by attaching the appropriate number of blue circle stickers to the bush shapes (or by gluing on circles cut or punched out of blue construction paper). Then mix up the cards and let the children sort them into pairs by matching the numbers of "blueberries" on the bushes.

Variation: Number the bottoms of paper baking cups and place them in a muffin tin. Then let the children put corresponding numbers of blueberries (or blue construction paper circles) into the cups.

Painting With Blueberry Juice

Drain the juice from a can of blueberries into a small bowl. (Reserve the berries for other uses.) Then let the children use the blueberry juice to paint designs on white construction paper or paper towels. Point out that while the skins of blueberries are blue, the juice is more of a purple color.

Variation: If you prefer using fresh blueberries for this activity, let the children help mash the berries with a fork. Then add a little water to extend the juice.

Blueberry Muffins

Sift together 1 cup white flour, 1 tablespoon baking powder and ½ teaspoon salt. Stir in ¾ cup whole-wheat or graham flour. Whirl together in a blender 1 egg, ½ cup unsweetened frozen apple juice concentrate, ¼ cup vegetable oil, ½ cup milk and 1 banana. Pour the liquid ingredients into the dry ingredients and mix well. Stir in 1 cup fresh or canned blueberries. Then spoon the batter into a well-greased 12-cup muffin tin and bake at 400 degrees for 20 to 25 minutes.

The Blueberry Bush

Sung to: "The Mulberry Bush"

Here we go round the blueberry bush,
The blueberry bush, the blueberry bush.
Here we go round the blueberry bush,
So early in the morning.

Pick the blueberries small and round,
Small and round, small and round.
Pick the blueberries small and round,
So early in the morning.

Additional verses: "Taste the blueberries ripe and sweet; Now let's make some blueberry (pies / jam / muffins / etc.) "

Elizabeth McKinnon

Moon Day

Moon Day on July 20 marks the anniversary of the first moon landing in 1969. The journey was made in the spaceship Columbia by three American astronauts — Neil Armstrong, Edwin Aldrin, Jr. and Michael Collins, who served as pilot. Neil Armstrong was the first to set foot on the moon, saying, "That's one small step for man; one giant leap for mankind." Then he and Edwin Aldrin walked on the moon for about two hours, where they planted an American flag, gathered rock samples and took photographs.

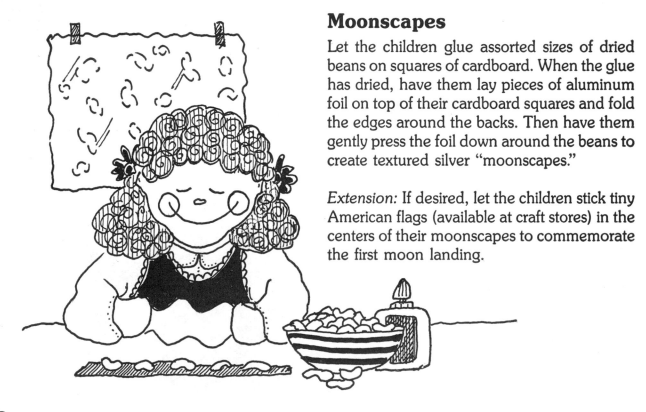

Moonscapes

Let the children glue assorted sizes of dried beans on squares of cardboard. When the glue has dried, have them lay pieces of aluminum foil on top of their cardboard squares and fold the edges around the backs. Then have them gently press the foil down around the beans to create textured silver "moonscapes."

Extension: If desired, let the children stick tiny American flags (available at craft stores) in the centers of their moonscapes to commemorate the first moon landing.

Trip to the Moon

Cut square face-holes out of the sides of paper bags. Let the children decorate the bags with crayons to make space helmets. Then have them put on their helmets and "blast off" for an imaginary trip to the moon. On the way, have them float around weightlessly in their space capsule. When they land on the moon, have them leap and float in slow motion as they pretend to plant a flag, collect moon rocks and take pictures of their surroundings. Then let them make the return journey back to earth.

Extension: In the lid of a shoebox cut four or five holes from small to large and set out a number of different sized rocks. Then let the returned "astronauts" sort the "moon rocks" in the shoebox sorter by placing each rock in the hole closest to its size.

Climb Aboard the Spaceship

Sung to: "Eensy, Weensy Spider"

Climb aboard the spaceship,

We're going to the moon.

Hurry and get ready,

We're going to blast off soon.

Put on your helmets

And buckle up real tight.

Here comes the countdown,

Let's count with all our might.

10-9-8-7-6-5-4-3-2-1 — BLAST OFF!

Let the children act out the movements as they sing the song.

Elizabeth McKinnon

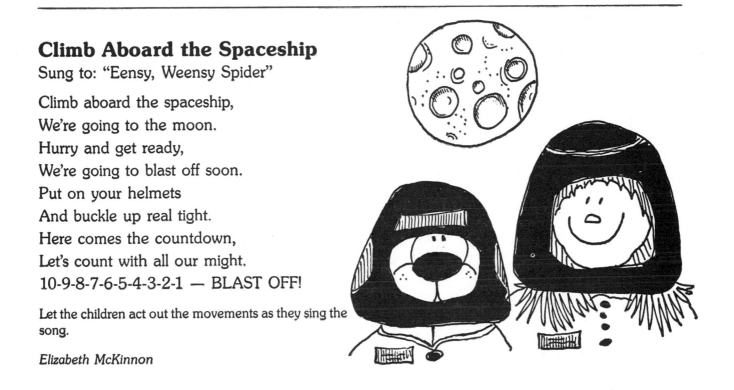

Vegetable Astronauts

At snacktime cut vegetables such as celery, cucumbers and zucchini into different sized chunks. Then provide the children with toothpicks and let them put the chunks together to create "vegetable astronauts." (Note: Have the children remove the toothpicks before eating their snacks.)

Variation: Use cubes of cheese instead of vegetable chunks.

Moon Day

Clown Day

Celebrate National Clown Week by having Clown Day any time during the first week in August. Besides doing the activities below, you might wish to set up a Clown Corner that contains clown books, puzzles, dot-to-dot pictures and other clown games. Include a box of dress-up clothes or clown costumes along with makeup and a mirror for the children to use for dramatic play.

Clown Hats

For each child make a cone-shaped hat out of colored construction paper. Let the children decorate their hats with materials such as construction paper circles, star stickers, yarn, rickrack and glitter. Let them glue cotton balls on the tops of their hats for pom-poms. Then attach yarn to the sides of the hats for ties.

Extension: Help the children put on their hats and attach small red construction paper circles to their noses with loops of tape rolled sticky side out. Then play circus music and let the children march around the room in a Clown Parade. Encourage them to act out clown movements as they march.

Flannelboard Clown Game

Make five felt clown faces with collars attached. Number the clowns from 1 to 5 by gluing the appropriate number of felt dots on the collars. Then make five felt clown hats and number them from 1 to 5 by gluing on felt numerals. Let the children place the clown faces on a flannelboard. Then have them match the numerals on the hats with the dots on the collars and place the hats on the clowns' heads.

Variation: Cut hat and collar shapes out of different colors (or textures) of fabric and let the children match them accordingly.

Did You Ever See a Clown?

Sung to: "Did You Ever See a Lassie?"

Did you ever see a clown,
A clown, a clown?
Did you ever see a clown
Move this way and that?
Move this way and that way,
Move this way and that way.
Did you ever see a clown
Move this way and that?

Have the children form a circle. Each time you sing the song, let a different child stand in the middle and act out clown movements for the other children to imitate.

Paula C. Foreman
Millersville, PA

Clown Face Salads

For each child place a scoop of cottage cheese on a small plate. Make clown faces by adding cherry tomato noses, green pepper ears, olive eyes, red pepper mouths and lettuce bowties.

Variation: Instead of vegetables, use a variety of fruits to create the clown faces.

Aviation Day

National Aviation Day is observed each year on August 19. This day honors Orville and Wilbur Wright, the brothers who made the first airplane flight in 1903 at Kitty Hawk, North Carolina. To celebrate, you might wish to display pictures or models of different kinds of aircraft — jets, propeller planes, helicopters, gliders and space ships. Or invite the children to bring aircraft toys from home to use for show and tell. For a special treat, you might wish to arrange a field trip to a local airport.

Airplane Stencils

Make airplane-shaped stencils out of lightweight cardboard and use masking tape to attach them to sheets of light blue construction paper. Let the children brush paint over the stencils, using any colors they wish. (The stencils can be used more than once. Just remove them carefully and retape them to clean sheets of paper.) When the paint has dried, let the children glue fluffed-out cotton balls on their papers for clouds, if desired.

I'm an Airplane

Sung to: "Oh, My Darling Clementine"

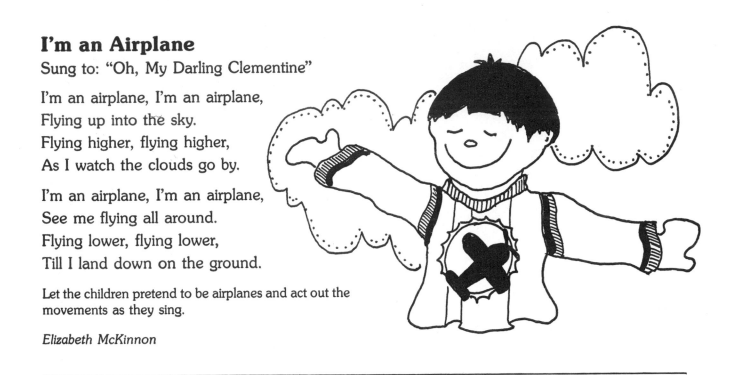

I'm an airplane, I'm an airplane,
Flying up into the sky.
Flying higher, flying higher,
As I watch the clouds go by.

I'm an airplane, I'm an airplane,
See me flying all around.
Flying lower, flying lower,
Till I land down on the ground.

Let the children pretend to be airplanes and act out the movements as they sing.

Elizabeth McKinnon

Planes in Their Hangars

On a sheet of butcher paper draw three large rectangles to represent airplane hangars. Draw one rectangle with a red felt-tip marker, one with a yellow marker and one with a blue marker. Cut out six airplane shapes each from red, yellow and blue construction paper. Mix up the shapes. Then let the children match the colors of the airplanes with the colors of the rectangles and line up the planes in the appropriate hangars.

Airplane Dining

For each child place snacks such as crackers, vegetable sticks and dried fruits in a TV dinner tray. Line up chairs, facing forward, in two double rows to make an "airplane cabin." Then let the children sit in the chairs while "flight attendants" serve them their snacks. The children can hold the TV trays on their laps while they eat.

Totline® Newsletter

Activities, songs and new ideas to use right now are waiting for you in every issue!

Each issue puts the fun into teaching with 32 pages of challenging and creative activities for young children. Included are open-ended art activities, learning games, music, language and science activities plus 8 reproducible pattern pages.

Published bi-monthly.

Sample issue - $2.00

Super Snack News

Nutritious snack ideas, related songs, rhymes and activities

Sample issue - $2.00

- Teach young children health and nutrition through fun and creative activities.

- Use as a handout to involve parents in their children's education.

- Promote quality child care in the community with these handouts.

- Includes nutritious sugarless snacks, health tidbits, and developmentally appropriate activities.

- Published monthly.

- Easily reproducible.

With each subscription you are given the right to:

Make up to:
200 COPIES per issue

Warren Publishing House, Inc. • **P.O. Box 2250, Dept. Z** • **Everett, WA 98203**

Totline® Books

Super Snacks
Teaching Tips
Teaching Toys
Piggyback®Songs
More Piggyback® Songs
Piggyback® Songs for Infants and Toddlers
Piggyback®Songs in Praise of God
Piggyback® Songs in Praise of Jesus
Holiday Piggyback® Songs
Animal Piggyback® Songs
Piggyback® Songs for School

1·2·3 Art
1·2·3 Games
1·2·3 Colors
1·2·3 Puppets
1·2·3 Murals
1·2·3 Books
Teeny-Tiny Folktales
Short-Short Stories
Mini-Mini Musicals
Small World Celebrations
Special Day Celebrations
Yankee Doodle Birthday Celebrations
Great Big Holiday Celebrations
"Cut & Tell" Scissor Stories for Fall
"Cut & Tell" Scissor Stories for Winter
"Cut & Tell" Scissor Stories for Spring
Seasonal Fun
Alphabet Theme-A-Saurus
Theme-A-Saurus
Theme-A-Saurus II
Toddler Theme-A-Saurus
Alphabet & Number Rhymes
Color, Shape & Season Rhymes
Object Rhymes
Animal Rhymes
Our World
"Mix & Match" Animal Patterns
"Mix & Match" Everyday Patterns
"Mix & Match" Holiday Patterns
"Mix & Match" Nature Patterns
ABC Space
ABC Farm
ABC Zoo
ABC Circus

**Available at school supply stores and parent/teacher stores
or write for our catalog.**

Warren Publishing House, Inc. • P.O. Box 2250, Dept. B • Everett, WA 98203